MARYANNE VANDERVELDE, PH.D.

Films and Friends

STARTING AND MAINTAINING A MOVIE GROUP

THOMAS DUNNE BOOKS

ST. MARTIN'S GRIFFIN ≈ NEW YORK

THOMAS DUNNE BOOKS.
An imprint of St. Martin's Press.

www.stmartins.com

Book design by Nick Wunder

Library of Congress Cataloging-in-Publication Data

Vandervelde, Maryanne.
    Films and friends : starting and maintaining a movie group /
Maryanne Vandervelde.—1st ed.
        p. cm.
    ISBN 0-312-32079-5
    1. Motion pictures—Societies, etc.   I. Title.
PN1993.V33 2004
791.45'06—dc22

2003061182

First Edition: January 2004

10   9   8   7   6   5   4   3   2   1

CONTENTS

ACKNOWLEDGMENTS

There have been nineteen members of our movie group over its seven years of existence, and I am grateful to all of them for their contributions to the fun, meaningful relationships and personal growth that I have experienced.

But the five people to whom I owe the biggest debt are, in alphabetical order: Dick Davis, Jill Davis, Susan Dykstra, Carol Farrell, and Ray Looney. Upon my first mention of this book idea (late at night, after lots of wine), these five people were immediate and enthusiastic supporters. They volunteered to help in whatever way they could, and they have contributed so much: ideas; research; publishing options; tough critiques—always lovingly offered; and lots of emotional and moral support. I will never forget the day that they all came to a meeting with their checkbooks, offering whatever money I needed to tide me along in this project.

There are other group members who have helped as well. Jim and Pam Going were not at the "launch" meeting, but they've been very helpful with marketing ideas. David Dykstra is the near-professional photographer who took the cover shot, and he is also our longtime recorder whose summaries were crucial to the chapter on the films we have seen. Chuck Farrell, the group's most prolific moviegoer, offered his packaging company to make boxes for special editions of this book.

I also want to thank the four people whose movie groups we heard about over the last couple of years and whose comments were helpful in enlarging this book beyond *our* group's experiences. And I want to thank the very diverse members of eight movie groups that our people have helped to start over the last three years. We have loved our roles as consultants and have been gratified by the enthusiastic feedback we continue to get from members of these new groups.

My terrific agent, Ellen Geiger, saw the potential in this book immediately and made many useful suggestions. And Carin Siegfried has been a wonderful editor to work with because she loves movies, appreciates the psychological complexities of groups, and anticipates the effect that more movie groups could have on the film industry.

Finally, I wish to acknowledge my husband, H. Ray Looney, and our son, Spencer Velde Looney. I have always loved movies as an art form and educational tool, but Spencer piqued my more critical and business-related interest through his film development work at Disney and elsewhere. He has very eclectic tastes and knowledge, and I am always fascinated by his opinions. Ray and I often disagree about movies (as well as other things), but he is a great sounding board and has been my supportive partner throughout this endeavor.

IT HAPPENED ONE NIGHT

Part 1

(GETTING STARTED)

CHAPTER 1

WANTS AND NEEDS

On many Saturday nights, our group members are "sleepless in Seattle"—not because we are lonely or lovestruck but rather because we are arguing into the night about the movie we have just seen. More important, we are bonding in a way that we have rarely experienced in other groups. For seven years now, this movie group has been a very important part of our lives, and we want to share our concept with the world.

LIKE—AND UNLIKE—A BOOK GROUP

When it began, none of us had heard of movie groups. Book groups, yes; some of us belong or have belonged to them. But most of us did not want to devote the time that book groups require or spend the money that current books cost, let alone repeat some of the unsavory features that book groupers talk about—having to read boring books chosen by others; putting up with people who come but don't read the books, people who monopolize conversations, or people who never open their mouths; tolerating a group that operates for many years without the members ever becoming friends because the focus is more on the books than the people.

Experts have estimated that there are somewhere between 250,000 and 750,000 book groups in the country—approximately eighty percent made up solely of women. But when we thought about a film group, we especially wanted to engage the men. Four of our male members are avid readers, but none has ever considered a book group, and they give three reasons for that:

▶ Every book group that they've ever personally heard of is populated by women. These guys say that, even if those groups allowed men, they fear that the groups "would be dominated by librarian types."

▶ Book groups seem to read mostly fiction whereas most men prefer to read history or biographies.

▶ They don't have time to read a whole book every month, especially if it is one that they have not chosen personally.

Our members, both male and female, assert that all of us can justify two hours and a $7 to $10 ticket, even if a film is lousy. It is more difficult to spend twenty or more hours reading a book and $12 to $25 buying it.

There is undoubtedly some special value in single-gender groups, but we, from the beginning, wanted the dimensionality of gender diversity. Many, perhaps most, of the movies we see contain gender issues, and, if the film doesn't evoke gender concerns, our discussion surely will. It's helpful to have balanced male and female perspectives on the film. Furthermore, it is easier to plan a weekend activity as a couple than as an individual—that is, if one is in a relationship.

Book groups range from small numbers supported by local, independent bookstores or libraries to the media-sponsored ones like National Public Radio. Of course, Oprah Winfrey singlehandedly advanced the concept of the power of reading by her encouragement to pick up a book and think about it. When she stopped her efforts, both she and her audience missed the group so much that it was restarted. She asks readers to consider change by focusing on issues that challenge prejudice and ignorance. But Oprah's audience is predominantly women, and her book choices reflect that. It remains to be seen whether Oprah or any of the other media book clubs will be able to interest more men.

Nevertheless, many book group concepts are very relevant to coed film groups, and we suspect that the gratifications are similar:

▶ fun and laughter;
▶ making new friends through ideas discussed;
▶ exposure to concepts that we never would have encountered otherwise;
▶ intellectual as well as emotional stimulation;
▶ making a good book or film last longer by discussing it with others;
▶ expanding our understanding of a book or film from idiosyncratic and simple to complex and multi-dimensional; and
▶ facilitating the human connection for which we all hunger and the unexpected possibilities inherent in that connection.

MEANING FOR US

What has this group meant to us? First, the intellectual and emotional stimulation has fulfilled a real need in our lives. Work settings are usually focused on prescribed areas, and competition there tends to prevent certain types of personal dialogue. Cocktail party–type interaction is almost always superficial. Family relationships are complicated and are driven by other-than-intellectual issues.

By contrast with most other groups, then, the movie group forces us to think critically and deeply. Sometimes it even leads us to emotional places we would rather avoid, but the outcome is almost always positive in terms of personal growth. It encourages us to listen to others' opinions and reevaluate our ideas.

Why has our movie group been the source of such meaningful relationships? Because when you talk about a movie, you talk about yourself. We didn't all know each other when we began, but we were amazed at how fast we truly became a group. Sharing is the key to all relationships, and we have *shared*. We now care about each other in a way that superficial friends don't, and we joke about a retirement home where we can rock together on the front porch while we talk about movies.

More than anything, however, our group has been great fun. We all look forward to it. We take pleasure in the food, the teasing, the camaraderie, catching up on each other's lives, and the whole mix we have developed. As an added bonus, many of us admit that our taste in films has changed. One man was overheard saying recently, "I wouldn't go to a movie like that crap anymore. It's all noise and no brains."

GENERAL MEANING

Friendship is a tricky thing. Many hard-charging career people do not take the time to develop friendships outside of work. Their colleagues are their primary friends, or they don't think friendship matters much as they climb the ladder to success. They have kids to raise, parents to accommodate, and things to do. Then, their kids grow up and leave the nest. Their parents die. They retire or are downsized, and they find that those work buddies may not have liked them very much after all. These life-changing events often leave people alone and lost.

Throughout our lives, many of us move and have to create our world anew. Having school-aged kids may help in a new community. Pets can help us meet people too. We try to make friends with coworkers. We find religious groups. We join volunteer organizations. But nothing could be better for making new friendships in a new setting than a movie group. People who've just relocated can simply ask two or three others—newcomers like themselves or natives—and the group will mushroom.

This doesn't mean, of course, that all is sweetness and light in a movie group. A good group gives us pleasure but also forces us to consider the place we make for ourselves vis-à-vis others. Occasionally there are painful consequences, but, as our parents told us, that can build character. After a meeting, some members will ruminate about their own behavior:

- ▶ Did I say something stupid?
- ▶ Did I divulge too much?
- ▶ Was I intolerant of someone?

▶ Can I accept those who don't have the same values or reactions as I do?

Or, on the receiving end:

▶ What did he or she mean by that?
▶ What do they really think of me?
▶ Are we finding the right balance between casual conversation and therapy?

The answers to all these questions require some self-examination and, in the best scenarios, our conclusions provide some learning about self in relation to others.

The deepest form of human interaction is recognizing something about oneself in another person. In this way, we form connections, which we clearly need for a healthy life. Of course, some people try to avoid risks in their interaction with others. Perhaps they have been hurt in the past and are overly vulnerable; maybe they never developed social skills. But there is no doubt that the riskiest forms of communication usually provide the biggest psychological rewards.

If we open up, others usually will too, and all involved participants will find interesting commonalities as well as differences. Discussing movies with friends has the potential to make those meaningful connections that medical science tells us we so desperately need for emotional as well as physical well-being.

Movies are fantastic vehicles for presenting every possible type of person, action, relationship, and situation. No single individual can experience all of these in reality, but movies have the potential to take us into all kinds of outside worlds. In addition, looking at movies introspectively can take us into *interior* worlds that we may not have examined before.

We recommend movie groups for young people. This could be a high school extracurricular activity, a boys' and girls' club event, or a new, fun challenge for college students as they move into a dorm or a fraternity or sorority house.

After college, young people need to invest in friendships outside of work because personal relationships are usually richer than work-based associations, which often have hidden agendas. Young alumni groups, church-related groups, professional associations, or simply neighbors in an apartment complex can work well as a base. Or there doesn't have to be any connection at all except a loose network of acquaintances.

We also recommend movie groups for mid-lifers. They need breaks from their kids and the pressures of heavy responsibilities. This is an inexpensive night out. It builds adult relationships. And it gets the brain cells working on something besides family and work.

And we certainly recommend movie groups for seniors because meaningful relationships at older ages are more important than ever. (As some brilliant thinker once said: growing old is not for sissies!) Couples or singles living in their own homes can organize a movie group independently. Retirement communities, assisted living facilities, even nursing homes can also help in putting a group together.

So, why do we want to share our experience? First, everyone to whom we mention the group seems fascinated, and many in the Seattle area ask to join. But, besides the eight groups that we've helped to start, we have heard of only four movie groups across the country. Although most people know of film classes, they have not heard of a leaderless movie group, and we feel strongly about equal participation versus the leader-driven, moneymaking kind.

Our group has evolved by fits and starts over seven years into a pattern that works. Other movie groups may as well not have to reinvent the wheel! We hope this book will trigger many more groups, more fun, and maybe some feedback that will give us ideas for a future edition.

SIGNIFICANCE FOR THE FILM INDUSTRY

Let's just be grandiose enough to mention here that movie groups could truly influence the kind of films that get financed and made. There is general consensus in the publishing industry that book groups have kept alive the mid-list books that otherwise might be ignored. Similarly, consumers in movie groups could affect the way in which Hollywood and its distributors make decisions. If movie groups thrive, we should get more intelligent, character-driven fare than we are offered today. Chapter 15 takes a closer look at this possibility.

CHAPTER 2

OUR BEGINNINGS

It started at a dinner party for twelve. Most of us had seen a hot, new film, but there were huge disagreements about what it all meant. At one point, there was so much screaming that some of us worried whether a fistfight would break out. Then, suddenly, we were all laughing about someone's insight. One woman, puzzled about the movie's relationships, asked, "How long do you think romantic love lasts?" Well, that question—and that evening—are remembered as the genesis of something pretty great.

A few days later, three of us women talked about how much we had enjoyed that discussion and how much we missed that kind of intellectual and emotional stimulation in our lives. It had almost felt like college, during which we'd stayed up all night talking about life. One of us suggested a lunch for most of the women who had been there to discuss taking this to another level. There was, interestingly enough, general agreement that one of the women present that night would not be invited. Her comments had been sarcastic and inappropriate. She just didn't fit!

In retrospect, we've wondered whether we should have included some men in that lunch. The gender issue periodically raises its ugly—albeit fascinating—head when one of the men feels controlled. Indeed, some debate about gender equity arose in the first meeting of the movie group. We now think that most of the men would have "owned" the group more from the beginning if they had been involved in the planning stage. But we didn't know where we were going with this, and a small group always makes decisions more quickly than a large one.

As it turned out, only three of us from the original dinner party were available for lunch on the appointed day, and all three were enthusiastic about proceeding. We decided to make some tentative rules.

(It should be noted that these are *not* our *current* rules. Some have remained, and some have changed. If you're looking for a prescription for starting a movie group, please go to chapter 12.)

INITIAL RULES

▶ *No more than fourteen in the group.* Most of our homes can handle twelve around a dining room table or living room, and often two or more people will be missing. On the occasions when we are all together, fourteen is a "squeezable" number.

▶ *It wouldn't matter whether group members were married, otherwise coupled, or single. We preferred mid-lifers in age.*

▶ *Participants had to like movies and commit to the process.* We agreed that there might be some trial and error here, but giving thorough descriptions of our plan to potential members would help. We three hoped our own partners would cooperate.

▶ *This was to be a leaderless group, so we wanted neither prima donnas nor shrinking violets.* We wanted to promote equal participation among group members.

▶ *Each of us would invite four or five people and then confer.* We would first invite the two women who had expressed interest after the dinner but were not at this lunch. We wanted an eclectic mix of professions and personalities. We started out with four married couples, two unmarried couples, and a single man. And we *are* eclectic!

▶ *We would meet on Saturdays, see a late afternoon movie together, and go to someone's house afterward. We would try to meet about once a month.* We found a date three weeks away to give people time to plan.

▶ *The host would tell everyone the movie choice and time at least a week early.*

▶ *Films currently in theaters would be the focus, as opposed to videos.* The experience of seeing a film on the big screen seemed important to us, and current films would allow us, if we wished, to gather professional review information.

▶ *We would only choose "discussible" films. Each host would have some obligation to do this, but hosts should not have to preview films.* Occasionally, hosts have chosen duds, but usually there is still something worthwhile to discuss.

▶ *Food would consist of "heavy hors d'oeuvres" brought by guests, with dessert, wine, and coffee provided by the hosts.*

▶ *We would not talk about the movie until we sat down for dessert and coffee.* This is often a hard rule to follow, but we enforce it on each other scrupulously.

▶ *At the direction of the host, everyone in turn would rate the movie from one to ten and tell why. Only after that would general discussion begin.* This rule was made because we thought we had some "engineering types" in the group who would sit back and not participate verbally. Well, were we ever wrong! It is often hard to shut people up so that everyone gets a turn! And, the best discussions are usually the ones where ratings go from very low to very high.

▶ *If any members were to be absent on a given night, the host could invite anyone to fill in. These could be try-outs for future membership. With the permission of the host, a member might bring houseguests.*

Of the people we invited, we had two turndowns. One couple was traveling a lot and asked to be considered later. Another couple sounded dubious about both movies and the time commitment, and we decided not to encourage them.

THE FIRST TIME

The first session was almost a mutiny! The hosts asked some of us to recommend films, and one of the women had just seen and loved *Antonia's Line*. As we were filing into the theater, the following comments were heard:

A Dutch film? In *Dutch*?

I won't read subtitles! Too much f_____ work!

All about women? *Three* generations of women?

Who chose this movie?

The social part of the evening went well as we enjoyed each other's food and got acquainted a bit, but the movie ratings went from two to ten. One woman, who talked about having just watched a friend die, hated the film and said that she was probably not in the mood to see something so heavy. One man raged about subtitles, but other people countered that the best films are often foreign. As the themes of *Antonia's Line* were brought forth, and as people shared their own experiences with family members and small towns, it became clear that all of us were learning from each other. We were also learning about each other.

At the end of the movie discussion, we talked about rules and heard some bitter resentment about their having been established by only three people. But, when the participants were told that this evening was our chance to change the rules, nothing major evolved. Just minor tweaking. This was also the opportunity for people to change their mind about membership, but no one did. Everyone seemed enthusiastic, and people quickly volunteered their homes for next times. We had started to set some new patterns. We had started to become a group.

THE RIGHT STUFF

Part II

□ SP   □ LP   □ EP   □ WHCP   □

(MAINTAINING AND CHANGING)

CHAPTER 3

CHANGES OVER TIME

PEOPLE CHANGES

Two couples have split up over these seven years. The single man and one couple have moved away. Another couple had a temporary overseas assignment, but they're now back, returning to the group when there was an opening. Three new couples have joined over the last four years.

So, how did we choose which part of a splitting couple to keep? The decision was a combination of their desires and our wishes. Usually, in this kind of group, one member of the couple has been more committed than the other has been. In one case, the remaining member subsequently lost her sense of commitment, and she has drifted away. In the other situation, both the man and the woman chose to leave in order to avoid difficult decision making. If ever there is a time for a group to be flexible, dealing with a divorcing couple is it!

How do we choose new members when there are openings? This has been a bit tricky. Some members would like a smaller group and have lobbied to *not* accept anyone new. But the consensus has been to replace departing members, so we have talked in great detail about possibilities—both formally (within the group) and informally (outside of it). Usually, the new members are people who have attended the group as guests, so we have all had a chance to meet them. If a member proposes someone we don't all know, we try to get the "applicant" to come as a guest. We have never formally voted, but some of us are more pushy than others, and there have been a few hard feelings. If two factions want different people to come in, and the group cannot arrive at a consensus, we suggest drawing straws for a "your turn/my turn" decision.

We are currently a group of fourteen, plus previous members who visit occasionally. We range in age from mid thirties to early sixties, but we believe that age, for the purpose of discussing movies, is irrelevant. Our group is diverse. We are mostly American-born, but one is British, and one came to the U.S. as a child from Greece. Most of us are college-educated, and several have advanced degrees, but three did not graduate from college. Most of us are married; four current members are coupled but unmarried. Of the total, only two couples are in their original marriages, although one second marriage is long-term. There have been several divorces among us, and three members have lost spouses to death. Most of us have children, ranging in age from teenagers to adults, and three of us are grandparents. We have observed that the two members who have no children sometimes react differently to films from the rest, and we find that fascinating. Our occupations include: stock trader; retired military; actress; college professor; small business owner; management consultant; corporate officer; anesthesiologist; attorney; mortgage banker; musician; homemaker; medical researcher; museum docent; orthodontist; and writer. Many of us are board members of for-profit or nonprofit organizations or both, and some of us do lots of volunteer work. Most of us are still gainfully employed; two are retired.

RULE REVISIONS

After a few months, we began to hear complaints about seeing the film together on Saturday afternoons. We had been trying to save seats for one another, and, in crowded theaters, we got lots of people mad at us. In fact, one couple had saved a whole row only to find that none of us showed up. They eventually learned that they were in the wrong section of a big multiplex.

Some people also were unhappy about giving up Saturday afternoons, when they would rather be doing other things. If we went to the late afternoon show, the evening was finished by around ten P.M., and the earlybirds were happy. However, if we kept Saturday afternoons free and went to the 7:30-ish show, we ended our activities past midnight. The night owls were happy with this arrangement, but the others started falling asleep.

It suddenly became clear to all of us that there really is no good reason to see films as a group. *Now the host notifies everyone of the film choice about a week ahead of time, and we all go at our leisure.*

We try not to be competitive about choosing good movies, but those who choose duds have to put up with a little complaining. We don't want people to have to preview movies, but some of us do. All of this puts some *pressure on the host to do a little homework.* And we have also learned over these seven years that *certain times of the year don't offer as many good choices in movies as other periods do.* For example, October through December is a great time to find a wealth of good films because the Academy Award contenders are often released then. Those films stay in theaters during January and February, but March and April can be difficult.

The food situation has changed, too. There were some male-type complaints that people weren't getting enough to eat, so we decided to plan dinners instead of hors d'oeuvres. For a while, the host usually made an entrée, and the rest of us volunteered for appetizer, salad, starch, or dessert. We experimented with different menus. One couple made a big pot of soup; some people barbecued. The food stayed casual for a while, but then we lapsed into "competitive cooking"—complete with linen tablecloths, sterling silver, crystal, and china. Eventually, some of us hated the pressure and the extra time that required, and we are now back to heavy hors d'oeuvres—although we did succumb to a fancy New Year's Eve dinner last year.

We also have a recording secretary. About two years into the group, we found ourselves asking one another questions like: What was that film about horses? What was our rating on that lesbian thing? Thankfully, one brave soul took it upon himself to reconstruct a list of all the films we had discussed, including when and where, and we all contributed by correcting his drafts. He now takes notes at every meeting—ratings, typical comments, etc.— and *sends us a newsletter by e-mail* with this info along with the next meeting time and place. These newsletters are great resources, to which we refer often.

Meeting plans have changed somewhat. From the beginning, someone has always pulled out a calendar at the end of an evening and initiated a discussion about the next time. Early on, we would agonize over trying to find a time when everyone would be available—preferably on a Saturday night. Perhaps we worried that feelings would be hurt if a meeting was planned when certain people could not attend. Now we realize that people are busy and some members may have to miss some meetings. We schedule times when most people are available, and we try to plan something once a month. We also have enjoyed experimenting with Friday and Sunday nights, and we've sometimes tried Sunday brunch. We like the casual feeling of a Sunday brunch, but Saturday night is still the time that most people prefer.

Also, we seldom met during summertime the first couple of years because of vacations. Now we meet quite regularly during the summer. In fact, the people who have retired are more likely to be away in the winter than summer. Fourth of July has been a special treat because one couple has hosted movie groups on their boat—with food, swimming, spectacular fireworks, *and* movie discussion.

We have struggled a bit with how to handle *people who don't see the movie or people who miss too many groups.* One clever fellow reviewed a movie quite brilliantly before tripping himself up with a crazy detail—then laughing and admitting that he had not seen it. We all enjoyed the humor, but when he tried it a second time, we landed on him. One couple has missed more groups than most, and they don't always have good excuses. They have been told, thus far jokingly, "three times in a year and you're out." Another couple is spending more and more time at their home in the sun, and we are trying to sort out the pattern.

CHAPTER 4

AS GOOD AS IT GETS

Describing what we do is tough. So, in an effort to get the flavor of the group, we recorded our discussion of *As Good As It Gets*—an Oscar-winning film with Jack Nicholson, Greg Kinnear, and Helen Hunt. This was an atypical critique in that most of the ratings were similar. But it is a good example in that it evoked some rather personal discussion and showed the comfort level we feel with one another. In many ways, this was an evening in which our interaction was as good as it gets. The names have been changed to protect the guilty!

Joanne [one of the hosts]: So, who wants to start?

Barbara: God, I just hope I can remember it.

Joanne: You go first then.

Barbara: Okay . . . I liked it. I didn't absolutely love it. So I would give it about a seven. I thought the performances were terrific. Jack Nicholson always plays himself, but he was great in this, and I thought Helen Hunt was good, and I loved Greg Kinnear. But I thought afterward: why does it take children and dogs to tell the story, to make us laugh and cry? I found myself wondering: would this couple stay together? Is there enough there for them to stay coupled? And I don't know . . . I kind of doubt it. I hate to start on a downer, but I thought the message is pretty scary that . . . this is as good as it gets. I mean, he used the phrase in the shrink's office. And I guess that was appropriate, but it's kind of a downer message. And for the two of them, it sounds like they were settling. I mean, they did complement each other, and that was lovely, and that's the positive side of the relationship, but the thought of what's ahead for these two people is pretty scary. But, well . . . that's also a positive lesson in a way because some of us have problems with wanting things to be better than they really are . . . and wanting perfection, and we can't have that. So, if you look at it from the other side, there's a positive message that we have to be realistic about what life has to offer. And this film was amazing in its ability to make us laugh one minute and be in tears the next. That is always fascinating in a film . . . that you can have that transition so quickly. So . . . it was good. I enjoyed it.

Carolyn: I just loved it. I'd give it a nine or a ten because . . . well, first of all, there aren't that many good movies. I thought that whoever wrote this script was excellent. It's amazing that the characters really did start out as absolute caricatures—you know, swishy gay guys, and a woman with a sick child, and a man who really couldn't function. And it was really amazing how people who start out like stick figures could change into really interesting people. I ended up loving them all for their own personalities. And what I really liked best about it was that each of them brought something important to the relationship . . . and that each of them worked together. They all helped each other. The three of them each gave the other two what they basically needed. And the casting was excellent. They were all very odd, odd people. But interesting odd people . . . like us. . . .

Jack: Now wait a minute. [Laughter and denials that we are odd.]

Carolyn [continuing]: But they really loved each other. And I think . . . a lot of what life is . . . the really important thing in life is having good friends. Even if we don't have much else, friends like you. . . .

Jim: We're not your friends. [Laughter from the men. Women insist: "yes we are."]

Carolyn [continuing]: Okay. I'm done. Larry . . . Oh, I'd give it a nine.

Larry: I'm sort of like Barbara. I'd probably give it a six. I just thought the facial expressions were great on Jack Nicholson—even though I never like him very much in movies. The last movie I saw him in was . . . What was the name of that thing where he pretended to . . .

Penny [Larry's wife]: Never mind. That's not what we're talking about now.

Larry: Okay, okay. So, we got to talking on the way home about why they were the way they were. Nicholson's father had been the same, I guess. And then the . . . the gay one . . . he was the way he was because he had to paint his mother nude. So we ended up in a big disagreement about why everybody was so weird. So, I guess that's about it. Everybody was too weird. About a six for me.

Ann: I'd say about a six-point-five. I think Nicholson is just one of those actors who grows on you. But Helen Hunt made me think a little of that sitcom. . . . I never liked her on that sitcom. She always seems to be very angry. So I never think of her as very upbeat. She always seems to play the same role—that same angry attitude. I think this role called for someone to be a little more warm and fuzzy, and I just can't see her that way. But, overall, it was a good story, and I really liked the Kinnear character. . . . So I guess I'd give it about a nine.

Others: What? Nine? I thought you said you didn't like it? What happened?

Ann [continuing]: I changed my mind while I was talking. [Laughter.] Nine, I guess. I like happy endings, and I guess it was a pretty happy ending.

Jack: I'd give it an eight-and-a-half. I happen to love Nicholson. Just looking at him makes me laugh. I could watch him in every movie. Even if it's not a great movie, it's just nice to have him around. But this was a pretty good story, too. I liked the changes in all the characters over time. I liked the Greg Kinnear character, too—found him very believable. It was not an easy role for him to play. He sure is good-looking.

Stan: Too many comments from you guys about the gay guy. You're making me nervous. [Uncomfortable laughter and snide comments about Stan's sexual orientation issues.]

Jack [continuing]: Yeah? Well, I really love Kinnear *and* Nicholson. [Fighting posture.] You want to fight about it?! And I thought one of the greatest lines I ever heard in my life was when he says that compliment to her about . . . you make me want to be a better man.

Others: Yes. That was fabulous. Really a good line. That was the best part.

Jack [continuing]: A couple of other things. And I agree with a lot of the things that have already been said. The thing with the dog was so great—the way that relationship grew. And, I don't know if you noticed or not, but the piano was not in tune.

Penny: Really? What was that all about?

Jack [continuing]: Well, he didn't have anybody to play it. And his life was kind of out of tune anyway. The best theme of the whole movie was when he walked out . . . when he says it doesn't get any better than this. Anyway, I thought it was great—an uplifting movie, and I enjoyed it.

Evan: It's a nine for me. I loved the device about not stepping on the cracks. It's so brilliantly visual, and it's something where you can show a change at the end. It's something I often have thought about as I walk down sidewalks. I used to avoid the cracks when I was a kid. . . .

[Laughter and accusations about which ones of us are that weird and how everyone will be conscious now about stepping on cracks.]

Evan [continuing]: The only other thing I have to say is that the restaurant scenes were great. His craziness about food made me really think about how our family has all this stuff about food. Everybody likes different things. My daughter won't eat until she smells the food, and then she pushes it around on her plate for a long time.

Ann: Maybe we should talk about what idiosyncrasies all of *us* have—when this is over.

Chloe: No time for that tonight. [Laughter.] It's Jim's turn.

Jim: I loved it. I think I enjoyed the relationship between Nicholson and Helen Hunt the most. And the way they changed . . . you know, the way she helped him to change. It started with the demand that *she* act a certain way, and that really pissed her off. Then she realized that this individual wasn't the man that she thought he was. He was intelligent and pretty caring. Then, eventually, he came to admire her, and he came to respect her, especially as he got involved with her family. So, they started out with all these problems, and then I guess he really did want to change, but he needed the shove to do it. She demanded, do it now! So then he was finally willing to try to make those changes. I thought it really was great, and I guess I'd give it a nine.

Jack: Now will all of our wives want to change us?

Several men: Of course. Nothing new about that. [Laughter and conversation about change and how it gets harder with age.]

Joanne: Hey, we have a lot more to go!

Stan: I'd give it a six. I had a little trouble early on relating to some of the people, and I wondered how the hell they were going to do anything interesting. I tried to figure out what the dog meant. I'm sure he was a major part of the plot. I just kept wondering how they went from making Jack that ugly to that loveable. Okay, Chloe, your turn.

Chloe: Well, last night when I saw this movie with Penny, we just couldn't resist talking about our kids . . . because thinking about all this in the context of your kids is a very scary thing. And I found it very interesting to think about the amount of obsessiveness that we have in our family. I don't even know much about this kind of illness, but I feel like I do now because a lot of my impressions of the world come from films. Like, first of all, I only know a few black people, so I know that my impressions of blacks have been formed largely by movies. And I don't know many people with disorders like this. So, the things that I hold true in my life . . . a lot of my attitudes come just because I've seen it in a movie somewhere. And that's begun to concern me because . . . for example, I realize that a lot of my attitudes about drugs have been formed by the movies. Sometimes I like that because there aren't too many other ways to learn about these things—other than the things I've learned in my family. But it might be dangerous. My biggest concern, really, is that I've become a little more cynical recently, and that reminds me a lot of my father. I used to wonder why he got so cynical in the years since I was young, but I now think that he was exposed to a lot in those years that I was not exposed to. What bothers me is that he is pretty racist, but I know that his opinions on race are different from mine, and I'm glad that I've gotten more open ideas about race from the movies. I guess, in many ways, my life was pretty sheltered, but now I think that seeing films has helped me not be so sheltered.

Larry: But don't you feel that movies are presenting, in subtle ways, both sides of racism—and that you as a viewer are expected to see both the commonality of this and the ugliness of it?

Chloe [continuing]: Sure, and I want to stay open so that I can see beneath the stated issues. . . .

Larry: Now, Nicholson was really an unlikable character, but he was meant to grow on you as you understood him more and saw that he had good in him too. Didn't you see that?

Jim: It's not your turn, Larry!

Chloe [continuing]: Sure. I guess that's all I have to say. I'll give it a seven.

Megan: This film will probably go down as one of my favorites of all time. I laughed so much, but I cried too. I just know that these two troubled people will make it together. They went through a lot to get together. They will surely find a way to make it work. I'm not always an animal lover, but I

did love the dog here. It was so important to the plot. I
could say more, but I don't want to repeat anything you all
have said. I guess I'll give it a nine.

Bill: I can't believe anyone gave it a nine! Most of these men
were really despicable people. The gay guys who did the
crimes belong in jail, but there was no assurance in the film
that they would get what they deserve. And Jack Nicholson's character—would you want your daughter ever
hooking up with him? He seemed very angry and quite dis-
turbed mentally. Even Helen Hunt hadn't done a very
good job of looking after herself and her child. I felt sorry
for her, and I laughed at Nicholson's crazy antics, but these
aren't people I can identify with. I guess I'd give it a five—
but only because of the good acting.

Joanne: Well, that's interesting. I really loved the movie, but I
dreaded seeing it because I didn't see how they could make
Obsessive Compulsive Disorder funny. I already knew a lot
about OCD because one of my brothers has it. And . . .
this film was *very* effective in the way it described this illness.
It really gave a very clear picture of the way these people
feel about stepping on the cracks, washing their hands,
socializing, and so on. For our family, it's better now, but it
was very difficult—especially for me. It's still very painful,
but what was hopeful for me was that the Nicholson character got better. My brother is getting over it, but it was
amazing how that happened for him. He just decided that he

didn't want to take the medication anymore. He doesn't have OCD now, but I must admit that I wonder if it could return. What was interesting in the movie was that he said that the medication only helps sixty percent of the population, and he started taking it because of her. And so, I thought that the relationship in the movie was limited if he did it only for her. In the beginning, they got together because of her need, but then she started to like the guy.

Jack: I thought she fell in love with him first.

Joanne [continuing]: I'm not sure. The love just started to grow. And the interesting lesson with the Helen Hunt character was that anything is possible. With a different mindset, you can do anything. In fact, that's what the person with OCD doesn't have—the right mindset. All these crazy things are very real for them. All that obsessive thinking . . .

Tom: That's what I don't understand. Can't you just explain things to an obsessive person?

Joanne [continuing]: No. OCD is a chemical imbalance. The synapses in the brain just don't work right. For most of us, we can handle anxiety. For some reason, this individual doesn't get the messages like the rest of us do. It's not clear what triggers these things. It's just like a depression. It can come out of nowhere.

Larry: There's a difference between liking to do something and *having* to do it. I guess OCD people don't know why. They don't just *like* to do it. They *have* to do it.

Joanne [continuing]: It's like some people just have to cross their legs at the table. Some people just have to wash their hands. And there are certain categories . . . some people just have an overload of obsessive compulsion. I have a friend who has to play chess all the time. If he doesn't play chess every day, he gets a migraine. I guess it's the same with some runners.

Jack: What about drug addicts?

Joanne [continuing]: That's a physical addiction. This is a chemical imbalance, and you either grow out of it or the medication can help in getting over it. So, when I first went into the movie theater, I was thinking, how can they make this into a comedy? But, gradually, it was so cute—really hilarious—so I guess I would give it a nine. I liked the fact that you could learn something from this movie.

Tom: I don't know what there is left to say . . . except that I loved the car trip. That ménage à trois was one of the funniest groups I have ever seen. The scenes in the motel were hysterical. I found myself kind of wishing that Helen Hunt and Greg Kinnear could end up together, but I knew that was unrealistic unless the gay guy was rewritten as straight.

Penny: But they were all great friends, weren't they? Just goes to show you that there's no accounting for why certain people care about each other. I guess it's chemistry . . . and shared experience.

Tom [continuing]: Yeah. Well, I guess I'll give it a seven.

Penny: Tough to be last, but I've been stewing about something. Did it bother anyone that Jack Nicholson is a good thirty years older than Helen Hunt?

[Some say yes; some say they really didn't feel the age difference.]

Penny [continuing]: Maybe we're just so used to seeing this on screen. But this is only one of the reasons why I worried about the ending. They were two needy people who might be able to make it together. But he's so much older . . . And how could he ever be unselfish enough to be a father figure to her kid? And could he really change enough to be more or less normal?

Carolyn: Isn't the key line the one spoken by the mother—something about just finding someone who won't go crazy on you? Oh, sorry, it's still your turn.

Penny [continuing]: I'm almost finished. The film *does* make you think about perfection versus as good as possible. I know I sometimes have a little trouble with that issue. [Laughter, especially from her husband.] I guess I will give it a seven-point-five.

Someone brought up the meaning of the silverware and how the repetitive nature of Nicholson's unwillingness to use silver from others drove the point home. Then, we talked about the meaning of the dog and how all three of the characters really bonded through the dog. Someone mentioned the great dialogue and the unusually subtle writing for a Hollywood blockbuster movie.

Penny wanted to go back to the older man–younger woman issue. One woman said that this pattern is probably because younger actresses are more attractive and will draw more of an audience. It's also because the older man–younger woman relationship is such a common male fantasy. This was denied by some men in the group but affirmed by others.

The women wondered why we, as females, don't have many fantasies about younger men. The answer: young men generally strike us as immature, and we don't have time to train them.

There was some discussion about Nicholson's career and the choices he has made, with a couple of people relating information about how much he wanted this role. Some people love his work; others can hardly stand to watch him. Facts about his personal life and his current relationship with a very young actress were mentioned.

Then a general discussion ensued about whether and how our evaluation of a movie is influenced by our feelings about an actor. Several people suggested that they would have given this film a higher rating if the Nicholson role had been played by someone else. And yet, everyone acknowledged that it was a tough role to get right, and that Nicholson has a real comic flair.

No one in our group was cynical enough to put the following spin on Nicholson's now-famous line:

"You make me want to be a better man, Olivia.
Then maybe I could find somebody else."

CHAPTER 5

EVALUATION TOOLS

Our group has no set formula for approaching movies, and we certainly do not want any member to ask formulaic questions during the discussion. But the following suggestions may help members of movie groups as they think about both films and groups.

THE MOVIE

With their verbal expressions and visual images, movies are rich platforms for discussion. In our experience, individual participants use all kinds of criteria for their evaluations, but, in general, most people find special meaning in:

- ▶ the storyline and the way it is presented;
- ▶ casting and the interpretations of material by actors;
- ▶ ways in which we identify with the characters;
- ▶ questions unanswered or troubling gaps;
- ▶ what aspects, if any, stick with us over time; and

▶ what it all means—to us as well as to others (reviewers, friends, etc.).

More specifically, we try to ask ourselves questions like:

▶ Did this movie work for me? Why or why not?
▶ Did the screenwriter do a good job of drawing the characters?
▶ Was there an early, full description of each character, or did a picture gradually emerge from telling details such as bits of speech, comments by other characters, clues from physical appearance, etc.?
▶ Did the characters seem real?
▶ Did I identify with them? Why or why not?
▶ Did the screenwriter create a setting that I found interesting?
▶ Did I feel as though I'd entered another world?
▶ Did I learn anything new by being there?
▶ If this setting is familiar to me, did it ring true?
▶ Was there a compelling problem or conflict at the outset that drew me in and made me want to know what would happen next? If not, did that happen more gradually, or not at all?
▶ What are the frictions in the story progression that create challenges, dilemmas, and controversies for the characters?
▶ How are these frictions familiar to me?
▶ What tone or mood does the screenwriter build?

- ▶ How does the choice of language help to convey this mood?
- ▶ Was the language spare or thick with description? Was it humorous? Poetic? Profane? Was it suitable to the plot?
- ▶ How did the language affect my feelings about the film?
- ▶ Were the visual images appropriate for the story? Did they enhance or detract from the storytelling?
- ▶ Were there any scenes of special beauty or effectiveness?
- ▶ Were there any major holes or unwarranted confusions in the story?
- ▶ Were there any contradictions in the storytelling or characterizations?
- ▶ How do I feel about the voice in which the story was told?
- ▶ If there was a narrator, did he or she have a special perspective that made me care about the events described?
- ▶ What was the point or theme of the story?
- ▶ Did it inspire me?
- ▶ Was the casting appropriate? How would I have cast it differently?
- ▶ Were there any brilliant actors?
- ▶ Were there any terrible actors?
- ▶ In what ways did the actors enhance or detract from the storytelling?
- ▶ Was the film directed well? How might I have directed it differently?

▶ Was the budget appropriate to the storytelling? Would the film have been improved by a bigger or smaller budget?

▶ Was this a movie that stayed with me for days or weeks afterward? Why or why not?

▶ To what other movies would I compare this one? How did this one stack up?

THE GROUP

Our members believe that the interpersonal aspects of a movie group are just as important as the film focus. The discussion of a movie can be a wonderful context for making human connections and for analyzing issues in our own worlds. But the group process aspects of movie groups are no less complicated than they are in any other collection of individuals.

The one constant of a movie group is the members. They are really quite brave. They are willing to expose themselves—revealing their reactions and tastes, with their biases and doubts and convictions, for public scrutiny. Sometimes they even reveal aspects of their background or attitudes that they never intended to divulge. Not every member dares to do this, but there can be great rewards for those who make this kind of emotional and psychological investment. The beauty of movie groups is that they are entertainment, graduate seminar, group therapy, and old-fashioned gossip sessions—all rolled up into one.

Like all groups, however, movie groups need structure, and here are some quick tips for keeping the group on track. (Some of these are expanded upon in later chapters.)

▶ Make sure that the group is leaderless and that participation is more-or-less equal.

▶ Keep any one person from dominating the group.

▶ Keep everyone invested in it. Be sensitive to anyone who is feeling attacked or left out.

▶ Try to plan times that most people can attend, and then deal openly with those who miss too many sessions.

▶ Carefully consider whether new members will fit, and try to get group consensus on replacement decisions.

▶ Find ways to help newcomers integrate into the group.

▶ Confront the divas—those who would like to monopolize the discussion or control the process. Every group knows who the divas are. If they are not "handled" by other strong members, the less diva-like people will slowly stop participating and attending.

▶ Demand more of the movie discussion than sweeping praise or condemnation.

▶ Alcohol can be a great social lubricant, but don't let people drink too much. DUIs—those who "discuss under the influence"—can impede the whole process.

▶ When in trouble, go back to your original purpose.

▶ Encourage hosts to choose movies carefully. Even if a film gets a low rating from the group, it should contain issues that are discussible.

▶ Be open to any given film's potential to change a life, but don't worry if your favorite doesn't hack it for somebody else.

▶ Listen, especially to the quieter members. If another

member seems to lack listening skills, remind him or her to pay attention.

▶ Be creative about directions that a discussion might take.

▶ Open up about your own life, and others will usually follow.

CHAPTER 6

GROUP PROCESS

As with all groups, a movie group will have its ups and downs. Some movies provoke certain feelings. Some evenings are affected by events in the larger world. Other meetings are influenced by experiences in people's lives. Sometimes, individuals are in strange moods. Occasionally, the group process is shaped by an ongoing conflict between two or more participants.

Interpersonal relationships and group process are arguably the best parts of the movie group experience. They are unpredictable. They force us all to be perceptive, flexible, and responsive. They keep our creative juices flowing. They stretch our coping mechanisms.

A few of the group dynamics that any group will experience over time can be labeled as follows:

ALL QUIET ON THE WESTERN FRONT

Sometimes we are all in a mellow mood. This seems to happen fairly often when we have not been together for a couple of months and have missed each other. Or, it sometimes happens when the chosen film has been sentimental. It has also occurred, for us, when a member of the group has suffered a serious personal tragedy. Even on these evenings, however, one or more members can be counted on to be feisty. And one or more members can be expected to be funny.

STAR WARS

We have our fair share of divas—male and female. None of us is a shrinking violet. There are nights when several people want to talk at once. There are times when a person insists that his or her opinion is more valid than any other. Sometimes a member will go on and on. In these cases, the rest of the group can almost always be counted on to control the wars. It may take a shorter or longer time to kick in, but we seldom let one person become the star for long. For example, there was wild disagreement about *Memento,* for which our ratings went from zero to nine. Those who didn't "get" the film were called "stupid" by one man who loved it. He then got verbally—and almost physically—attacked by others, and he smashed a wineglass by holding it too tightly. The moderate peacemakers eventually prevailed.

THE USUAL SUSPECTS

We know one another so well by now that some of us are pretty predictable. Those people are often teased when their film ratings are as anticipated, but they are razzed even more when the rating is higher or lower than expected. "Oooh, Joanne liked the sex in this one." "Wow, a chick flick that Jack could actually tolerate."

BEAUTY AND THE BEAST

These episodes are part of the gender wars. They are usually set off by a gender issue in the movie that one woman or one man verbalizes and reacts to. Then a person of the opposite gender gets his or her back up, and a fight ensues. It turns to fun when other men and other women jump in. It feels most uncomfortable when the disagreement is between just two people and gets prolonged by one or both of them.

RASHOMON

The most interesting discussions occur when participants see the film in three or more ways. In fact, someone frequently makes the comment, "Did we see the same movie?" This happened with *Being John Malkovich,* which held profound meaning for some, was incomprehensible to others, and was just plain silly for the rest. Usually, by the end of the evening, we have hashed things out to the extent that there is a general consensus about meaning—but not always. Some of us seem to want to achieve agreement and closure, while others are fascinated by differences. Most of the time, when we cannot see one another's point of view, we can agree to disagree.

THE THREE FACES OF EVE

There are times when one participant divulges something quite secret and private about his or her personal life, and the whole group is shocked. The members are almost always supportive and almost never accusatory, but it sometimes creates tension when others don't know how to react. Eventually, it creates closeness as the group feels privileged to be let in on a confidence, but it can temporarily cause confusion about who this person really is. Sometimes, one member seems to have a split personality—coming across differently on given evenings. For example, one man who is usually open and generous can occasionally be closed and nasty. The group is a bit on edge about him, wondering which personality will appear on any given night.

THE WILD BUNCH

Sometimes, for no known reason, we have raucous evenings—loud voices, lots of drinking, strong opinions, dirty jokes, and conflicting reviews. Some of us love those evenings; others hate them and complain bitterly about what is going on.

THE ROYAL TENENBAUMS

Some nights we are like a really dysfunctional family. We love and hate one another at the same time. One person may make a very cutting remark, and later he or she may apologize profusely. Once we were considering a trip together, and one man said: "Why would I want to go anywhere with this crazy group?" There was a long pause before someone suggested that we may not want him anyway, and everyone laughed. Others then began speculating about places they wanted to visit.

SOME LIKE IT HOT

We have seen some very erotic movies, and some of our members love to talk about sex. Others find sexual subjects quite uncomfortable. Some are moralistic about extramarital affairs, while others do not feel at all judgmental. Some have gotten into their own sexual experiences a bit, while others always clam up about their own history. As we've gotten to know one another better and better, more sharing has occurred about sexual subjects because our experiences do truly color our attitudes about sex in movies.

A STREETCAR NAMED DESIRE

There is some flirting in our group, and we imagine that there would be a lot more in a movie group composed of singles. We seem to have found a comfortable level of good-natured teasing. We all glow when someone of the opposite gender likes something we are wearing or compliments a new hair style. "You look great tonight" is always appreciated. Only once, to my knowledge, did somebody cross our imaginary line with a sexually suggestive remark—which was basically ignored by everyone. It would truly be difficult if an affair were to develop among group members because it could interfere with the casual intimacy we feel for one another. It could even decimate the group if people had to take sides. We think an affair is unlikely to happen in our group because we have become a family, and our members are undoubtedly aware of the "incest" taboo among family members.

THE MATRIX

There have been nights when we really can't figure out what is going on. One person gets his or her nose out of joint about something. A given couple seems to have had a big fight just before they arrived. The host couple seems angry—maybe about the food we all brought, perhaps about a last-minute cancellation, maybe because someone asked to bring a houseguest and it was hard to refuse, possibly about anything else. In those cases, we may ask directly what is wrong, but, without a satisfactory answer, some of us (usually the women) burn up the telephone wires the next day, trying to validate our perceptions.

TWELVE ANGRY MEN

We seldom split male-female on movie discussions, but this division has occurred on the few occasions when the men think that the women have changed one of the rules without consulting them. The women tend to call one another regarding food, so they may also discuss the movie choice. Once, when a woman chose a film without consulting her husband, he and all the other men in the group ganged up on her at the meeting! Once, the majority of men complained about "too many chick flicks," but when the men were asked to choose the next movie, they picked a relationship-oriented film. Our changes from heavy hors d'oeuvres to dinner and back to hors d'oeuvres occurred because the men wanted it thus, and the women remind them frequently of the men's power. The women keep threatening to leave food preparation to the men, and some of them now participate more than they used to, but most of the men bring take-out when their partners are sick or out of town.

FIGHT CLUB

Once in a while, two of the members get into a macho, "pissing" contest (regardless of gender). They both try to prove how tough they are, and neither will back down. This can happen while we're having drinks, during dinner, or in the movie review and discussion time. It is usually about a stupid, inconsequential subject, but it often suggests a basic personality conflict. It can end with one or both of them stopping it by agreeing to disagree. Or it can end with the rest of us making remarks like "stop it" or changing the subject.

SIGNS

Sometimes there are mysterious signals that things are not right with the group. A couple of members may have repeated conflicts. One member might start to act weird, becoming a bit isolated from the rest. There are various ways for the other members to figure it out—either within the group or outside of it, but it can take a little effort. More often than not, an individual member has something going on personally and is trying to sort it out. Time and tolerance will usually resolve the difficulties, but intervention and support are sometimes warranted. The trick is to be sensitive to privacy concerns, while making it clear that other members are willing to help. For example, most of us loved *Secrets and Lies,* but one woman's review was quite convoluted. When pressed about her rating, she got tears in her eyes, and the rest of us backed off. Almost an hour later, toward the end of the evening, she talked about the child she adopted, the ethnic mix of that child, and the ambivalence she has always felt toward that child. The tears really came then, but the group had had no clue about the reasons behind her strange behavior until she opened up.

APOCALYPSE NOW

We no longer worry about our group ending because of some silly intolerance or disagreement. But our first session had overtones of a meltdown when the ratings for *Antonia's Line* went from two to ten and the men complained about three women making all the rules. Any new group should probably expect some volatility until the group really coalesces—until people learn that the group can tolerate some discomfort and still be a caring entity. Indeed, most members will learn over time that a group is usually strengthened through conflict that is solved constructively. But even mature groups can be threatened by the acting out of one or two people if the rest of the group members do not handle the process well.

BONNIE AND CLYDE

The group works best when couples come to the process as individuals—that is, they don't insist on sitting together; they haven't discussed the film with each other; they don't always give similar ratings; and they don't always defend each other. If couples seem to work only as an entrenched team, they would be boring in this kind of group. But a stranger walking into our group would probably know fairly soon who the couples are—not because they couple up, but rather because they handle each other so well. We like it when one half of a couple tells the other to shut up and give someone else a turn or to get to the point. One couple, in fact, uses the symbol of hands joined in an A-shaped point to tell each other to move on verbally, and the rest of us laugh when we see the signal.

WHO'S AFRAID OF VIRGINIA WOOLF?

What we don't like is a couple using the group to try to annihilate each other. Some partner squabbles are entertaining—even a catalyst for the rest of us to share our couples' issues. But one couple in our group, who later divorced, were vile to each other. And two other couples really had relationship problems, both now much improved through therapy and other means. All couples have their ups and downs, and the group has generally been tolerant of couples going through a bad time. But, if issues are never resolved and negative feelings persist, everyone else feels uncomfortable.

BLACK HAWK DOWN

Sometimes, by design or by accident, one member gets wounded in the group. A couple of our members are rather fragile and insecure, and some of our thicker-skinned members can be insensitive. More often than not, put-downs occur in a humorous vein, but they are not always received that way. Our group has become extremely adept at rescuing one another psychologically—often with an attack on the attacker; often with support of the wounded person's position; sometimes with telephone calls or lunches in the ensuing days.

MINORITY REPORT

It is fascinating how often one or more people will take an off-the-wall position about a film. In fact, a few of our members relish the devil's advocate position. Usually, this kind of discussion is fun—the cause for lots of good-natured ribbing. If it is a well-thought-out argument, it becomes the source of probing questions. If the person with the unusual idea seems quite fragile, he or she usually gets some support—or at least interest. But if the rest of us think that person is hopelessly bonkers that night, we are pretty good at confrontation. And if there is no possibility of agreement, we resolve to live and let live.

UNFORGIVEN

Only twice have there been incidents that were not forgiven easily. One involved a former member who was often absent and in other ways distanced himself from the group. We were all glad to see him go. The other involved two members of the group whose personalities clash. They got into a humdinger of a fight one night that took months to repair. They now tend to avoid each other physically, but they both work at nipping any conflict in the bud. The whole group can see progress in their efforts to become friends again.

DIE HARD

We have a couple of aggressive members who always want to win. They hate having their review criticized, and they interrupt the comments of others. But our group has become incredibly good at managing those who get out of line, and we have seen tremendous progress in some people as they learn to contain, and perhaps even change, their own feelings. For example, two men thought that the cross-dressing of the star in *Boys Don't Cry* was unrealistic. The group tried to tease them out of their extreme positions, but they got increasingly defensive. Finally, one man joked about going out for a beer with his buddy to support each other after the meeting.

TO BE OR NOT TO BE

It has sometimes been hard for new members to break into this tight-knit group. We have sensed some reluctance or standoffishness at the beginning about whether this kind of commitment has enough of a payoff. Furthermore, most of our members forego other invitations for the appointed movie group night, but a few members will accept another invitation if it sounds better. The totally committed among us have to accept some who give in to other priorities, and we know from experience that the longer people are involved in the group, the more they seem to love it. We try to remind new members that the original group did not all know one another when we began. We also try to get to know new members outside of the group—inviting them to one-on-one or couple-on-couple events.

GOOD WILL HUNTING

Although the movie by this name refers to a person named Will Hunting, these words aptly describe what most of us seek. It is a rare thing to find meaningful friendship with people who are also intellectually and emotionally stimulating. Sharing information about oneself in the context of movie discussions seems to work well for creating and solidifying relationships. Women are stereotypically known for petty jealousies, and men are usually seen as competitive and emotionally closed, but a group like this seems to diminish the worst in both genders and encourage the best.

YOU CAN COUNT ON ME

The best aspect of our group is the friendship. We feel that any one of us could count on any other person in the group if we had a personal crisis. Although most of us are pretty strong people, we always support a vulnerable member if he or she is inappropriately attacked. And these supportive feelings spill over outside of the group too. We haven't, to my knowledge, tested one another by asking for money, but the five people who offered me money toward this book made a lovely gesture. We have celebrated one another's birthdays and anniversaries. We have gone to one another's parties, weddings, and charity events, and we've thrown showers for one another's kids. We have taken food, sent cards and flowers, or called when one of us is sick or has had a death in the family. We have given one another all kinds of information. We clip newspapers and magazines, cognizant of one another's interests. We have traveled together, once as a group and often as couples, and we talk of future trips. We bring little gifts from visits to faraway places. We really care about one another.

CHAPTER 7

APPLIED INSIGHTS

One of the amazing byproducts of our film club is the spillover into our relationships with others outside of the group. This seems particularly significant for the group members who would not otherwise be going to these types of films or having these types of conversations about them.

CHILDREN AND PARENTS

It is sometimes difficult for older people to talk to younger ones, and vice versa. Mid-lifers and seniors want to impart their hard-won wisdom (or what they think is wisdom), but young adults clearly do not want advice. Most young people feel that only they understand current times and values. They think their parents and grandparents are hopelessly out of date. Both sides of this generational divide may want the other to listen, but neither side does much to bridge the gap, and both sides hate being lectured. If communication between kids and their parents is too much about either side, we promote selfishness and turn the other side off.

This divide can be bridged, however, and movies are a great vehicle for intergenerational communication. How cool parents are to their twenty-somethings when they have seen, and can intelligently discuss, a hot new foreign film! And how fun it can be for a kid to show that he or she cares about the parents' interests by suggesting a film that the parents might like! Even disagreements about the merits of a particular film can bring parent-child communication to a new, more positive level.

Some parents use their kids as movie consultants, and it seems to be a role they enjoy. It is common in our group for someone to say, "Jeremy told me that . . ." or "I chose this film because Heidi loved it." Over time, most parents and kids have gotten to know each other's taste, so recommendations are usually valid. One son recently said, "Dad would like this film, but it's probably too violent for you, Mom." That young man has said in the past, "This is a violent film, Mom, but the story is so good that you'd probably like it anyway." The same son has also taken movie suggestions from his parents. When both mom and dad loved the director's cut of *Cinema Paradiso,* the son was persuaded to see it. He and many of his friends ended up loving it too, saying that they were glad they didn't miss its short theatrical run.

Films can also be good family activities together. Most of our group members have found that their children actually enjoy attending movies with them, perhaps because we are more knowledgeable about films than most parents are. Indeed, if Thanksgiving or Christmas/Hanukkah holidays get too intense with family time, a movie can be quite the ticket—choosing it, going in a group, and discussing it afterward.

Generally, discussing a film can be a source of nonthreatening dinner conversation with family members. Thus, when things start to get a little hot in the parent-child (or child-child or parent-parent) interaction department, it's usually safe to move the discussion on to a comedy that one has seen or wants to see.

Fortunately, movies can also be a vehicle for getting into heavy stuff. For example, one son had recently told his parents that they were too controlling. The parents went to see *In the Bedroom* and recommended it to him. At first he resisted, but they joked about being controlling and maneuvering him into seeing it, and he eventually did. He loved it, as they had—but for different reasons. He, of course, related more to the son, while they focused more on the parents. Together, they compared their family to the one on the screen. They talked about seeming permissiveness from parents versus passive-aggressive control. The parents talked about how easy both their son and the movie teenager had been in adolescence. They also pointed to a couple of anomalies in their son's teenaged behavior, and they talked about how frightening those incidents had been for them. The son talked about why he could not relate to that character being sucked in by the needs of an older woman and her children, but he could imagine other situations that might lead a young man into trouble. The parents used the tragedy in this film to tell their son how important he is to them and how horrible it would be to lose him. They all talked about their fears of random violence. Then, the three of them compared their differing ideas about revenge, and they learned interesting things about one another.

Other parent-child discussions were provoked by *Life as a House*—a story in which Kevin Kline plays a divorced father dying of cancer. His angry, defiant teenaged son refuses at first to help build his father's house, but the whole family gradually heals over one summer as this construction takes shape. One couple in our group, both previously divorced, used the movie to discuss—with different children at different times—how hard their divorces had been for their children. Even though the film is a bit sentimental and sappy, they were able to get two of their four kids to open up in unprecedented ways.

Another adult child of two group members urged her *parents* to see *Life as a House*, and she then talked about her fears of losing one or both of them through death. The family took this impetus to do some estate planning, and all of them signed health care proxies.

So, what could be a bigger pleasure with adult children than getting to know them as separate-yet-close friends—and as interesting human beings? Discussions about movies are a perfect vehicle for this.

Several of us have overheard our adult child describe the movie group to someone else. It is often with humor about our take on sex or "bad language." Sometimes it's with surprise that we saw a particular film and maybe even liked it. At times, it is an idea they are considering with their friends, and maybe they want our advice. Almost always, it is with pride that the parents are still stretching the gray matter and trying to understand what others think.

At the other end of the spectrum, a few of our group members have parents in their sixties, seventies, or eighties, and some of these parents are quite lonely. We often hear stories about how useful movies have become in these parent-child relationships as well. For example, a member may suggest a film we have loved or may see it a second time with a parent. One woman took her mother to see *Shine* the week after we reviewed it, thereby reviving her mother's interest in playing the piano. That mother is now taking piano lessons again—after sixty years! And she bought tickets for the whole family to attend some symphony concerts together. The only downside is that she keeps insisting that her daughter should resume her piano lessons as well!

WORK ASSOCIATES AND OTHER FRIENDS

Movies seem to be seeping increasingly into modern culture, and it is interesting how often watercooler talk turns to films. Since our own work colleagues have learned about our group, we are often consulted as experts: "Did your group see this movie?" "What did you think?" "What's good out there?"

In other group situations like dinners and cocktail parties, people seem to love hearing about our novel idea. They ask for details. They ask about personalities. They ask about specific films. They ask if they can join. And we enjoy passing along our special passion about films and movie groups.

With friends and colleagues, as with family members, movie discussions are somewhat safe topics in an environment where many other subjects are not. Some people are quite comfortable getting into religion, politics, and other "taboo" subjects in a casual social setting, but many of us avoid these subjects like the plague in polite company. Couching these issues in the context of a movie is much more fair game. Almost all our members have experienced a social conversation that was made more interesting by our description of a movie group review. For example, three months after we had seen and discussed *American Beauty,* we compared notes about how frequently that film had come up in our interactions with friends, family, and colleagues. Most of those discussions had gone quickly to Kevin Spacey's lust for a teenaged girl, eliciting a wide variety of opinions on whether that quality is genetically ingrained or culturally taught, acceptable or totally reprehensible. Reporting these experiences of our group members in unrelated social conversations brought an added dimension to our discussion that evening.

Most people are busy and don't want to waste time seeing bad movies, and many people don't trust individual critics after having been repeatedly burned, so our members have become a source of information for people who trust our taste. That is, many of our friends and colleagues like to hear about our range of ratings and opinions, and they have come to trust the overall taste of our group.

There is a huge contingent of middle-aged people who, for various reasons, no longer see movies, but some of our friends have started going to theaters again because of our influence. Other friends have reawakened their movie interest by renting videos and DVDs. Because our members have become known as film aficionados, we find that we are often asked about past as well as present film choices. Sometimes, months later, we are berated or thanked for our advice.

At the very least, we are seen as having an unusual passion or hobby, and hence as a bit more interesting than we might otherwise be. Perhaps we even *feel* a bit more accomplished because we have learned skills in both critical thinking and group interaction, as well as having gained more knowledge about films.

CHAPTER 8

THEATER VERSUS VIDEO

We really prefer seeing current films in theaters if at all possible. Some of our members, who at first thought they would like the comfort of renting a video and watching it at someone's home, have changed their minds. The reasons for our theatrical choice are as follows:

First, the big screen and surround-sound are multisensory experiences. Simply going *out* makes it special—a time for which one has to plan and arrange logistics. Then, the community experience of laughing and crying with others cannot be psychologically underestimated. Our group members have talked about how different it feels to catch an unpopular movie midweek with only a few others around us versus sitting in a crowded theater, and we much prefer the latter. Furthermore, details are more visible on a big screen than a small one, and one of the most interesting parts of the group experience is learning details from others that you didn't see—or hear.

Second, we like having current reviews available. Some of us pay attention to reviews before we go to a film; some of us like to go cold and then compare our reactions to those of reviewers; some of us never look at reviews and criticize those who do as people who can't make up their own minds. Nevertheless, we all like knowing that we *can* look at many professional opinions in newspapers and magazines or on the Internet.

Third, we like being up on the latest films. It's more interesting to discuss a film currently in the media than one that came out years ago—especially when talking with our hot-shot, mile-a-minute, young-adult children. More than once, we have heard one of our kids say, "You saw *that*? I'm impressed." Furthermore, today's media are more filled with movie information than ever before—business stats on Monday mornings; relationships between movies and current events; gossip about stars. We want to know what's going on in the entertainment world, and current films help us to do that.

Of course, one can also make a case for watching videos:

▶ The choices are almost unlimited.
▶ One can stop and start the film—especially if something is unclear.
▶ Some people have big-screen TVs—almost as big as small theaters.
▶ There is comfortable seating at home.
▶ Less time is needed for coming and going.
▶ One can drink or eat simultaneously while watching the film.

Furthermore, videos make sense for groups that are concerned about cost. Just as a lot of book groups will only read paperbacks because they are cheaper than hardcovers, movie groups may prefer $3 to $5 for a rental versus $70 to $100 for ten people's theater tickets.

Convenience and location may be another issue for:

▶ people who want to stay close to their young children;
▶ people affected by bad weather much of the year; or
▶ people who live a long way from big cities and either have no local art theater or find it impossible to watch anything but blockbusters in their small town.

Our group did try a video experience once. We were in Palm Springs for five days together and decided to see two or three films during that time. We found one good movie in a theater that we had not seen, but two was too big a challenge for that small town. So we did a little survey and evolved a short list of old films people wanted to see—either again or for the first time. The couple responsible for that evening chose *The Four Seasons* with Alan Alda and Carol Burnett. The evening was not a bust, but its success was limited by:

▶ people not seeing the small TV screen well enough;
▶ verbal comments during the film—which wouldn't be made in a theater;
▶ eating and drinking—accompanied by movement and noise; and
▶ people who didn't like the film walking out.

We probably won't do that again! But if we do decide to watch a video together, we will need a bigger screen and some stricter rules for our more undisciplined members.

CHAPTER 9

GENDER ISSUES

Men and women are different! We may not be as different as Mars and Venus, but a coed movie group presents many great opportunities for exploring our differences—hopefully without nastiness or violence.

When a film group includes heterosexual couples, it is always interesting to discuss whether the man or woman chose the film and why. Nothing is more revealing about a couple's power issues!

One question we've wrestled with is: Do men and women like the same type of movies? The answer in our group is: yes and no. Since it is mostly couples who host and choose the movie, people are always making assumptions about who made this particular choice. Generally, women do pick relationship movies while men choose action ones, but it is not so easy to generalize in our group. The men seem to have learned that complicated, discussible stories are much better than mindless shoot-'em-ups. And women seem to have found that there are new worlds to discover in subjects like crime and sports. For example, all the women were amazed at how much they loved Denzel Washington's film about football and race, *Remember the Titans*. It received our highest rating ever, and it was about much more than sports.

"I understand completely. I like good movies, and you like bad movies."

Another question that interests us is, Do women and men rate movies in the same way? Many of us have been surprised by how seldom our gender groups think alike, as well as how much our ratings are hard to predict. There are a couple of people in the group whose opinions we think we know well, but even they surprise the rest of us sometimes. A film can spark something unpredictable in any of us.

Perhaps the primary gender difference is in tolerance for violence. There are two or three women in our group who usually accept violence in the context of a good story, but there are another two or three who always hate it. Gratuitous violence offends some of the men as well as most of the women, but the men clearly tolerate it better. Is it a macho characteristic that men will not let other men see them as weak? Or do boys grow up seeing and accepting more violence than girls? Or do male testosterone, human history, and evolution simply equip men with more interest in violence than women have? We are still pondering those questions.

Our group's experience with the Russell Crowe film *Gladiator* is illustrative. The ratings went from one to ten. Although the ten came from a man, two women rated it eight or nine. Both of these women loved the pageantry and history, and they were not put off by the violence. Three women rated the film very low, and the other ratings were mid-range. One woman said that the film only showed man's inhumanity to man, and she hoped that these are not man's natural inclinations. If so, governments should be putting antitestosterone drugs into the water supply.

Beyond film-related judgments, gender differences are interesting in decision making about the group. We periodically struggle with—and have fun with—issues of control. We have mostly chiefs and no followers of either gender in our group, and both the men and the women love to gang up on each other. Three women did actually initiate the group, and, because our women plan the food, they tend to do the calling about dates and movie choices. All of this sometimes translates into our men feeling that they have a lack of input, and they are not shy about expressing concerns. Actually, because this subject is openly addressed—usually with humor—we seem to have evolved a quite equitable sharing of roles. One man always barbecues at his house. One fisherman often shares his bounty. Most of the movie reviews are researched and reported by the men. Our secretary and newsletter writer is a man. Our periodic photographer is male. Come to think of it, maybe the women should begin feeling out of control!

CHAPTER 10

NO LEADER ALLOWED

Most major cities offer some kind of structured movie discussions—often sponsored by the groups that run film festivals; sometimes formed by enterprising individuals. Some of these sessions also include sneak previews of new releases.

There is money in it! We've seen prices as high as $39 per session in Seattle and $460 for a ten-session course in New York. The major advantage of these groups is so-called expertise. The audience listens to one or more experts, and the major process for the participants is ingestion.

One adult education class was described as follows:

> Film is the dominant art form of the current century, yet most of us watch without enjoying the thematic riches hidden in every film. By analyzing and discussing film clips, we'll catch the nuances and subtexts in movies. Learn to identify the elements of cinematic style, recognize the director's vision, and understand the visual language of film. With the guidance

of an expert, analyze a scene or two from film classics. Learn film terms and receive a list of The Best Movies Ever. Take this class and be better equipped to evaluate everything from the summer blockbusters to the Nightly News!

Another class was advertised as follows:

Come meet fellow movie lovers and participate in lively discussions of current films. Examine themes, characters, and stories. Get together with the instructor to watch and compare current films. Discuss likes, dislikes, and the feelings those films provoked. Make new friends, see new films, and share ideas in this eight-session class. Movie fees are not included.

A third group was described thusly:

Once a week you will preview a new feature film, after which the director or star will, in a lively interview, help us explore the ways in which technique and imagination blended to create that film. The exchange between the facilitator and guest is penetrating, candid, and often unforgettable.

There is nothing wrong with these commercial groups, and it is very possible for movie-lovers to attend both this type and their own group. But we believe that we have taught one another to do most of what the experts do—without paying for it. And we think having a leader has many *dis*advantages besides cost.

First and foremost, we enjoy forming our own intellectual challenges more than we do absorbing professional expertise. For this reason, even though some people in a group may be more knowledgeable about movies than others, it is *crucial* that the group *not* allow anyone to get into a leadership role. We want all members to think critically and show leadership at different times. If one person in a purposely leaderless group begins to take charge, others will sit back and resent it, and eventually they will probably drop out. The group can and *must* control this, even if it is not immediately apparent to every member how to go about the task.

We think that actual film education should be only a part of the learning process in a movie group. Between newspapers, radio, TV, magazines, and the Internet, all of us have access these days to many experts. But we want to do more than ingest. We want to form our own opinions, then share them with others, get feedback, listen to others' analyses, and perhaps modify our own ideas. This is unlikely to happen in a commercial group.

We also think that group interaction is just as important as the film education—if not more so. This is not the easiest part, but it is by far the most rewarding. It is hugely satisfying to engage with like-minded friends about our lives in the context of the larger world. It is useful to learn, with others, about fictional people facing challenges and conflicts because we can often apply these lessons to our own lives.

It takes a little work to form one's own opinions and sometimes defend them. It takes some tolerance and effort to really listen to others—especially when they occasionally can seem so wrong. It takes courage to get into socially taboo subjects like abortion, homosexuality, mental illness, even death. But good things result. We add spice to our lives. Unexpected friendships form. We grow.

CHAPTER 11

FINDING GOOD FILMS

So, how does one find a satisfyingly mature film? (We hate the fact that pornographic films have usurped the "adult" label.) These days, we don't find big studios making many intelligent movies because of the current economic structure. But, thankfully for many of us, good films can still be found.

Admittedly, they are not easy to find in small towns because it takes a fairly large population to support art theaters. But any decent-sized city has at least one theater showing good films—and often these are the most historic, interesting, funky, beloved theaters in town. Furthermore, when a small film gathers momentum and gets excellent reviews, the multiplex may deign to show it.

If you live in a small town and are usually dependent on videos or DVDs, you might want to take a group movie vacation to New York or Los Angeles. They get new releases before any other city and have a great variety of films in theaters. Or, take a group vacation to attend a film festival. They are proliferating around the country, but some festivals are better than others.

And please don't shy away from foreign films. Other countries, which seem to have sensibilities other than exclusively making money, produce some wonderful films. Some countries, like France and Australia, actually fund filmmaking efforts so that small, noncommercial films can get made. Many people attend film festivals simply because that is the only place where they can see many foreign films. Translations are never ideal, but one can get into the habit of reading subtitles fairly easily. You can help yourself by simply choosing a spot in the theater where your eyesight works best.

"When I heard that 'Charlie's Angels' raked in over forty million in its first weekend, I sensed that there was great confusion in this country."

You will find that the quality of movies can vary according to the time of year. October through December is best because that is the time that distributors bring out most of their Academy Award contenders, and many of these are held over in January and February. Next best is probably May and June. The mindless blockbusters start coming out in June, but good films can also be found in the summer months when some distributors "counterprogram" character-driven films against the big, adolescent-geared ones. Maybe they realize that the adults need *something* to see.

Reviewers can also help us find the films that we will like. We can make it a habit to watch critics like Ebert and Roeper on television. Their half-hour show each week is syndicated, so sometimes one has to search for it, but they make it a practice to review both the well-known and the more obscure films, American and foreign. Take notes when you watch Ebert and Roeper for future reference in theaters and video stores.

You will probably find less value in most other TV reviewers. They usually seem more interested in being cute than in being profound. But sometimes one can find a gem of a review on commercial or cable television.

Read other critics in newspapers and magazines. Most large papers have an entertainment section—usually on Fridays when the theater listings change. Read and clip reviews. Learn over time which local reviewers you usually agree with. And, if you think that one reviewer is consistently off the mark, make your feelings known to the entertainment editor and try to get that critic replaced. Pay attention to newspapers that list the reviews of several other papers. This won't give you details, but it will average out any one local opinion.

The Internet also offers us a wealth of movie information. There are many sites that showcase a specific critic, others that collect a multiplicity of reviews, and each of us, as an individual consumer, comes to rely on certain sites. Web sites for the two major Hollywood publications—*Variety* and *The Hollywood Reporter*—can be very helpful. The Internet Movie Database (www.imdb.com) or the American Film Institute site (www.afi.com) are both worth consulting, but the value of specific Internet sites changes drastically from time to time.

Any single review may not be reliable. Similarly, the previews or trailers that are shown in theaters can be very misleading. And, for heaven's sake, don't rely on hype or publicity. In fact, there may be an inverse correlation between the amount of advertising and the quality of a film. Many studios now inundate the marketplace with advertising for a bomb that needs a first-weekend success in order to earn back some of its astronomical cost before it fades quickly from word-of-mouth. They count on consumers not reading reviews that first weekend.

Nevertheless, with a little effort, good films are out there to be found. At some periods, in fact, there are too many wonderful films and too little time.

CHAPTER 12

JUST TRY IT

WHEN

We have found that meeting once a month feels about right. With time out for the busy December holidays and vacations in the summer or winter, we end up meeting about ten times a year. That means that enough time has elapsed so that we enjoy catching up with one another, yet not so much time has passed that we've lost touch.

Saturday nights still work best for us, even though we no longer try to see the movie together. Everyone is most relaxed on Saturday, and those who travel a lot on business are more likely to appreciate this timing—not just having arrived home or being about to leave when we meet. We have tried Friday and Sunday nights when there is not a Saturday that all of us are available, and it seems that Fridays are a little more laid-back than Sunday nights, when there seems to be a need to stop early. The best alternative to Saturday night, perhaps, has been Sunday brunch. This time frame has a different but very comfortable feeling, and, in nice weather, we've enjoyed sitting outside.

The host sets the time. Since our group includes both morning and night people, someone is always complaining. One night owl spends every Saturday afternoon working on his house and would prefer to start the group quite late. Another man gets up routinely at five every morning and starts to fall asleep after nine P.M. We try to compromise.

Our pattern for starting time seems to be about six P.M. in the winter and seven P.M. in the summer. Usually the group breaks up about eleven, although we have been known to go well past midnight.

As we have become a tighter and more loving group over these seven years, we look for ways to be together on holidays. Two Fourth of July events on a boat have been all-day affairs—with swimming, adventurous side-trips in a dinghy, fireworks, and red, white, and blue food, as well as movie reviews. Our three New Years' Eves together have lasted, surprisingly, until two or three A.M.

Getting out our calendars at the end of an evening seems to work best for planning, and we usually try to set two or three dates ahead. If someone finds that he or she has a conflict a week or two before a given date, the host may give permission for that person to call around, trying to find an alternative date. This falls under the flexibility department, but it seldom works with busy schedules.

Some of us get together at other times as well. When new people have entered the group, we realize that breaking into such a tight enclave can be difficult, so some of us try to see new people separately. There has been one wedding of group members who had been engaged for many years, and all of us attended. There have also been children's weddings, anniversary parties, and other family shindigs. Most of us are involved in charities, and we invite each other to auctions and other fund-raisers. But we try to be sensitive about expectations for any monetary involvement from one another.

And we also do not feel that everyone has to be invited to everything. Some of us go to theater, jazz, or the symphony together, but we never feel that we have to include everyone. We like getting to know one another—and one another's friends—outside of movie group, and we try not to be jealous when we hear about something in which we were not included. Of course, we all maintain other friendships outside of the group as well.

We find ourselves talking about vacations a lot, and some of us have traveled together. Indeed, one member offers immediately to give us her credit card number so that we can sign her up for anywhere we are going. At one point, when we found that several of us had reasons to go to Palm Springs, we planned five days in December when most of us were able to commit. It was a whirlwind time of golf, tennis, and hiking, with two nights for movie groups. We included, in these movie evenings, friends that several of us had in the area—teaching them our systems and preferences. One evening we had a group of thirty, and it was great fun, albeit hard to control.

We know that we are compatible, and we have this unusual movie focus, so we look forward to a cruise or other travels together as more of us retire. Who knows? The joke about a retirement home might become a reality if we could work out the many legal and logistical kinks. We certainly care about one another.

WHERE

We met once in a private room at a new Italian restaurant we were all dying to try, and we've talked about a fondue restaurant or a private club to which some of us belong. We know of one other movie group that meets weekly at a pizza restaurant after they see a film. We like the idea of nobody having to worry about the food.

But the most comfortable setting is still a home. Whether we scrunch around a dining room table to eat or stand up to nosh, we all look forward to sitting somewhere together for the discussion. And whether the setting is a large home or a small apartment, the group process is always more important than physical plushness. We have gathered luxuriously in a 7,000-square-foot house, and we have perched on floor cushions in a 1,000-square-foot apartment. Both occasions were equally joyful!

FOOD AND WINE

Two of us do not drink, but beer and wine are important to the rest of us. Perhaps they lubricate the social interaction. Maybe they help one's sense of humor. Undoubtedly, the discussion part of the evening is more fun and more caring because our emotions are more available by that part of the evening. On the other hand, too much drinking can be a deterrent to intelligent discussion, and some groups may have to turn off the liquor supply at a certain point in the evening. DUIs— those who discuss under the influence—should be discouraged.

Food is a complicated matter. Some of us are more into fancy table settings and gourmet cooking than others are. The women say that they do not want to spend a lot of time at this task. They joke about an evening when only the men would cook. Sometimes we do bring hors d'oeuvres or salads from the grocery store. We liked the winter evening when the host simply provided a pot of soup. But some people like to entertain competitively, and the rest of us can easily get sucked in. It seems that, just after someone uses linens and crystal and an elegant menu, the level escalates. Our decision to go back to heavy hors d'oeuvres (finger food) last year worked for a while, but two people said recently that they miss salads. Others hate to eat standing up. For now, each host in our group will choose the food plan.

We have heard of one group that likes to coordinate the menu to the movie, such as homemade tamales for *All the Pretty Horses* and Greek food for *My Big Fat Greek Wedding*. If gourmet food is important to you, go for it. But, if the psychological aspects take precedence over the gastronomical ones, we recommend that the group be casual about food.

REVIEWS

We strongly recommend a process in which everyone rates the film from one to ten and tells why. Even though our group had none of the hesitation about involvement that we planners had predicted for certain people, this rating system gives every member pretty even responsibility and opportunity.

We have wondered about the effect on one's evaluation from others who have previously talked. There is no doubt that we are often influenced, so we sometimes hold up "evaluation fingers" (one to ten) simultaneously. Our ratings are recorded, and then we go around the group and tell why. When we do this, we find that about a third of the members change their ratings during the discussion. This is neither good nor bad but simply an interesting phenomenon of reviews.

Another system we have tried involves writing our number review on a piece of paper, putting it in the middle of the table, and then assessing at the end whether we have changed and why. It has been interesting to talk about the factors that influence us in our reviews.

Recently, those who can't be at a movie group meeting have been sending their reviews through an intermediary via e-mail, FAX, or a telephone call. When one half of a couple must be absent, he or she usually sends a rating through the partner. We all seem to want to get our two cents' worth in.

In our group's assessments, the preferred position to talk seems to be the middle—not the first, when one must organize thoughts quickly, nor the last, when it is hard to be original. But, with the host assigning positions arbitrarily, we all get our turns at all positions over time.

One beauty of these discussions is that we usually get our questions about the film answered. We clarify our impressions and see things that we may have missed. Another advantage of the group process is that we get to assert our ideas and influence others. We also learn by hearing the opinions of others and having our own judgments challenged. On the best evenings, we both teach and learn.

Not only have individual members evolved over these seven years, but the group has changed too. We found it fascinating when one woman said recently that she thought our review of *Breaking the Waves* would be quite different today than it was five years ago. We would be looking for, and reacting to, different things than we did then. We would have more perspective. We might not be so offended by the violent sex because we would be more tuned in to the story content and context. Some learning about movies *and* ourselves has obviously taken place.

Still, the most interesting evenings tend to be those in which there is wide disagreement, with ratings all over the place—and with someone asking whether we saw the same movie. It's always fun trying to figure out why we're seeing things so differently.

One of our biggest challenges has been to contain members who talk out of turn or who tend to be verbose. Spouses often do this task, but the rest of us do it, too. Someone suggested that we get a three-minute egg timer and make sure it's in front of the usual offenders when they start to speak, but we don't want to resort to childish tricks unless absolutely necessary. And we certainly don't want anyone's participation to become stilted or regimented. A group like that would be no fun at all!

We have a couple of people whose ratings can never be a whole number. They like to get into the decimal points with ratings like 7.25 and 9.2. Everyone gives these members a hard time about being indecisive, but they persist.

RECORDING

We didn't start with anything as formal as a secretary, but we have enjoyed—and we highly recommend—making a record on which to look back over time. This can be as simple as:

- ▶ name of film;
- ▶ names of major actors and director;
- ▶ date;

▶ place of meeting;

▶ each person's rating; and

▶ average rating.

But we also like to add:

▶ interesting comments made about the film—positives and negatives; and

▶ decisions about the next meeting(s).

(See a form for recording on page 193.)

Sometimes our secretary hands out these summaries at meetings, but he usually sends a newsletter by e-mail or snail mail. Most of us then file them for our personal records. It helps that the recorder usually brings his file to the meetings so that questions like "What was that film we saw on the Fourth last year?" or "How did we rate *Gladiator?*" can be answered. Ideally, this recording job should be shared, but maybe you'll be lucky enough to have a perpetual volunteer as we do.

PEOPLE

Nothing is more important than the people mix. It will never be perfect, and it would be dull if we were all alike, but members should be selected carefully. Great diversity might be fun in a movie group, and there can be advantages in getting very different perspectives on films, but we think that there are also benefits in having people who are not *too* different. If the age range is too great, people tend to have different historical perspectives and reference points. If members' education levels and socioeconomic status are *too* varied, there will probably be more tension. Similar backgrounds probably help to facilitate the honesty and empathy that group members should expect from one another.

At minimum, the requirements should be:

- ▶ people who understand the concept of a movie group;
- ▶ people who are willing to experiment with different types of films;
- ▶ people who are open to new experiences;
- ▶ people who will commit to attending most sessions;
- ▶ people who can and will make intellectual contributions;
- ▶ people who can and want to get along with others;
- ▶ people who have a sense of humor;
- ▶ people who are willing to be challenged; and
- ▶ people who are open to personal growth.

We have a couple of members who are scary-smart. Once in a while, the rest of us feel intimidated by them. But we have learned over time that the smarties have lots of emotional vulnerabilities, just as the rest of us do. We know that intellectual talents (IQ) are not the same as emotional intelligence (EQ). Some of our members are very athletic. Some are musical. We have pockets of knowledge in all kinds of areas. We all have our strengths and weaknesses.

The initial formation of a group takes a little planning and discussion. It might start with a small core of people who know one another, but this is not absolutely necessary. A movie group can start with just one person who gathers a few friends or acquaintances. It is quite possible that movie group members will never be good friends, but the focus on movies should at least allow them to stick together. Since *our* members have benefited so much from the group process part, we obviously hope for more than toleration of one another, but not every person in the group has to be perfectly matched.

How do you choose new people when the group is already formed? If possible, bring them in as guests once or twice and see if they fit. Then, make sure that it is a group decision and that everyone has had a chance to express opinions. If there is a conflict between possible choices, and a consensus cannot be reached, draw straws or flip a coin—this time my friend gets in; the next time there's an opening, your friend is first in line.

What if you made a big mistake? What if, for example, a new member turns out to be arrogant and domineering? What if someone is always negative or condescending? There are ways to point these problems out to the individual privately—perhaps through his or her closest friend in the group. It is possible that that person can change, but perhaps it's more likely that he or she will choose to leave the group. We are all adults here, and we all have experience in pushing away a person who doesn't fit. This is not a governmentally regulated body. We don't want to waste our time. If worse comes to worst, the group can form a consensus that the host will simply not invite that person to the next session. But we want to be sensitive, too. The group should find the kindest way to deal with this kind of situation.

CHAPTER 13

YOU'LL LIKE IT

So, what can you expect to get out of all this preparation and effort? The benefits can be subsumed under three headings.

FUN

Movies are, arguably, our most interesting cultural phenomenon. They're a multibillion-dollar industry, and many American films are seen throughout the world. Practically every popular publication writes about them. The business press keeps track of profits and losses. Whether we attend movies or not, they seep into our subconscious mind. Many of the expressions we now use originated in a film, and common street-slang always ends up in a movie somewhere. Films give us historical perspectives on the past; they reflect and comment on many aspects of life as we presently know it; and they imagine and predict the future.

The best films also teach us about new worlds. They immerse us in some place or activity about which we knew little. They allow us to share in experiences we never would have encountered otherwise, and they introduce us to people we will never meet in other ways.

Much of this is available in books, of course, but movies add visual images to the words. Sometimes they add music or costumes or special, fantastical effects as well. They present all kinds of stories and characters. Movies are always group efforts—in contrast to books or art or music, which are usually created by one individual. They may be years in the making. They may be produced at astronomical cost by some larger-than-life moguls, who are taking huge business risks, but they can also appear out of nowhere on a shoestring budget. Their writers are often creative geniuses, and their directors are like generals of armies. Actors in movies are talented people whose private lives often become known to us. What a combination of factors to play with!

Middle-aged people who have stopped going to movies are missing a lot of fun. If we pay attention to the reported story content as well as the reviews, we can find many films that warrant our attention. Besides worthwhile American films, foreign sensibilities are very interesting to watch. The big screen is much more sensual than videos or DVDs watched in a TV format, but most of the fun parts of movies can also be gleaned at home.

In addition to the actual movie discussions of a successful group, you may find that there are peripheral benefits in spending holidays or traveling together. For example, our Palm Springs trip was a further bonding experience because it was interesting to relate to one another in a different way, in a different space. At some point in the future, our group may attend a film festival together. Some of us have been to festivals in Seattle, New York, and Park City, Utah, and those of us who went to Sundance in mid

January will never forget it. The PIBs (People in Black) and their cell phones were ubiquitous and amusing, and the panels of experts were very educational. But the films and their subsequent Q-and-As with filmmakers and stars were the real rewards.

For people who are not used to looking at movies for the purposes of assessment and group discussion, there is pleasure in learning a new skill. For those who like being in the know, it feels cool to be up on the latest films. For those who have always loved interesting movies, it is wonderful to have a forum in which to share ideas about them. It is a special treat to have others on whom to test our theories and questions: "What did it mean when she said . . . ?" "Wasn't there a gap in . . . ?" "I don't understand why . . . ?" "How would these characters really end up if they . . . ?"

Movie group members can feel a sense of accomplishment that the enterprise is their own baby. They put it together, and only they can make it work. In the best scenarios, the members understand one another and have become comfortable together—the best aspects of a family.

And the humor flows naturally in this context. For example, most groups can spend hours on sexual innuendo, and our movie group is no exception. Even though *Indecent Proposal* was made before our group began, we seem to return periodically to the question, How much money would it take for you to have sex with an ugly man or woman? Everyone thinks Demi Moore's character's decision to sleep with the Robert Redford character was too easy. What if he or she looked like . . . ? (We've had fun filling in the blank.)

MEANINGFUL RELATIONSHIPS

When a group like this is really working well, movies provide an indirect way of forming close and caring relationships. It's not like a therapy group because we don't focus directly on one another—although some of us have gotten help with personal problems from the group. It's not like a class with competition for a grade—although there is some competition in the way we exercise our gray matter. It's definitely not a cocktail party or dinner event, at which we would try to make superficial conversation and avoid anything controversial.

Instead, we learn things about one another here that we never would have known from other social settings. Who would have guessed that a serious, psychologically burdened tax attorney ran a dance hall during college? How else would we have known that the most seemingly lighthearted person among us lost both parents when she was very young?

Most of us have few opportunities for this special type of communication. Some of us crave it more than others do, but all of us benefit from it. We never know when we will need friends who will come through for us—who know who we really are and care about us anyway. These real relationships seldom develop if we are not real ourselves, and, over time, this kind of group will not let us be anything but real. If we try to be evasive or deceptive, other members confront us. They force us to be more honest and clear about everything in life.

Of course, not all group members will be capable of the ultimate in analytical thinking and personal exposure, and sometimes both men and women have to be allowed their facades. We have to meet people where they are, intellectually and psychologically.

Tolerating and appreciating differences is, surely, a learnable skill, and there can be something endearing about someone vastly different from you still caring about you.

Women have the reputation for needing closeness more than men, but our experience in this group suggests that the men reach out to one another as much as the women do—both inside and outside of the group. Perhaps this kind of experience makes it more comfortable for men to like and trust one another. Men in our group now ask one another to go skiing or fishing, play golf or tennis, or go to sporting events or to the movies—often when their partners are uninterested or out of town.

The best word for relationships formed in this kind of crucible is *rich*. There are very few opportunities outside of family to test, learn about, and share with others in any real depth. Practically any subject is safe in our group—even politics, race, religion, abortion, euthanasia, drugs, homosexuality, parents, and kids. People may not agree with you, but they'll usually be honest. And, because they care, they'll try to be helpful. What more can one ask of other people?

PERSONAL GROWTH

Films allow us to be voyeurs into worlds that we would not otherwise visit. They give us permission to spy. Sometimes this is exciting; it can also be very frightening. Some of these worlds are wonderful; others are horrific. But all this exposure makes us aware of our own reactions, values, and attitudes. And when we talk about our take on a film, we are usually divulging—purposely or not—meaningful aspects of our most private self. Other group members may help us in reinforcing our own ideas, or they may urge us to think differently. Indeed, there have been a few epiphanies among us over these seven years—both of the reassuring and the unnerving kind.

Most people lead pretty mundane lives. We can only be in one job, one romantic relationship, a few friendships, and one or two hobbies at a time. Most of us like predictability in life, but it is probably healthy to also appreciate the different worlds we see in movies—because life seems to throw a lot of change and unknowability at all of us over time. Movies can expose us to real-life and fictional characters, to true situations and fantastic circumstances. They can help us become more flexible—more able to understand the complications of life.

One of our members remarked recently that rigid boundaries make him unable to think. His mind shuts off when he is really constrained. He said that analyzing films, with their different genres and stories and characters, makes him feel more alive. Being challenged by friends in this group context has helped him to grow.

Change is hard for all of us, regardless of age. Outside of therapy, we have few opportunities to look at ourselves critically. In our everyday relationships, it is easy to think that others have agendas—which they often do—and to dismiss their critical observations. Somehow, however, in this kind of group, there is little incentive for vindictiveness or tearing down. Instead, we tend to support one another in contemplating change. As we've come to know one another better, behavioral patterns have become more clear—patterns between partners; patterns in relating to the group; patterns of thinking. We've learned that some of us are quite cynical or angry. Some of us are very naïve and gullible. With humor and a light touch, we have all been told how we come across. Our task is to listen and possibly change—if we want to and if we can.

For example, one man in our group is politically far to the right. His positions create controversy, and he used to become even more extreme and defensive when he was confronted. Then, we have a man who is equally far to the left—always has been, always will be, he says. Lately, however, both men seem to be more conscious of their verbal content and timing, and it might even be possible that their ideas are becoming more mainstream. These two have had some vicious arguments about capital punishment, abortion, and other things, but they have gradually become the best of friends.

In another example, two women came into the group hating any film that contained vulgar language. They have struggled to explain why this bothers them so much, while others for whom "bad" language is not necessarily value-laden have made efforts to describe why not. Language, these members contend, can be uniquely descriptive. It can help explain the characters and story. We have all acknowledged that our reactions to language stem from our experiences in our families and elsewhere. And what an interesting way this has been to hear about one another's childhood and work experiences! Both of these women still prefer "proper" language, but they have become more accustomed to all kinds of verbiage and can now focus on other aspects of a film.

Films have given the men in our group an opportunity to explain to the women how the world forces them to cover up their feelings, and the women have told the men why females are sometimes overly emotional. We've talked about nature versus nurture, and we've argued about how much change is possible in personality traits like anger. A recovering alcoholic in the group has helped us understand that disease better, and he is quick to point out instances when film portrayals of alcoholics do not ring true. People who have adopted children have helped all of us understand that experience better. One buttoned-down manager plays drums in a smoky jazz club some weekends and has told us stories we can hardly believe about his experiences. In so many ways, we have learned about and from one another.

One woman recently told another, "You are an example of 'what you see is what you get.'" The second woman's response was, "Does that mean I'm transparent? Superficial? Is that a compliment or an insult?" It's a big compliment, said the first, who added that there is great value in facing the world with the attitude, "I'm okay; you're okay." Most of us know that our most difficult and most rewarding task in life is to accept ourself and others as we really are, and the group process of a successful film club can help us accomplish this task.

Who would have guessed that amateur film criticism could be a kind of Rorschach or Myers-Briggs test! For some of us, the group has truly been a vehicle for lifelong friendships and significant personal growth.

CHAPTER 14

VARIATIONS ON THIS THEME

We know of four other movie groups around the country, and we have, to date, helped in starting eight more.

The groups we know of started in different ways from ours and have evolved with different processes:

▶ The Matinee Idlers are a group of ten men in the Los Angeles area who have been meeting for about eight years. They are all retired. They started as a hiking group but turned to movies when two of them had trouble walking. They get together every other Wednesday for lunch, followed by a movie that they choose that day by consensus. If the film has been interesting and provocative, they discuss it over a beer afterward. If not, they just go home. In the early years, one of them occasionally brought his wife or girlfriend, but the group eventually put an end to that. They do allow visiting children to join them occasionally. As they get older, they have helped one another out with medical resources (one of them is a nonpracticing physician) and legal issues (one is an attorney). They say that they never fight and they expect to be friends forever. They dread the day that one of them is disabled or dies.

▶ A coed movie group in Kauai, Hawaii, has been meeting for twelve years. They are mostly single and middle-aged, and the group size has ranged from six to fifteen. They gather on the first Friday evening of every month, and they take turns choosing the film. They may go to any of the three theaters on the island, although that means a long drive for some. They always go to a pizza place near the theater to discuss the film, and they often close up the restaurant. They have few rules; they simply go around the table giving opinions. When people drop out and the group gets small, any member can invite someone new, but they never want to get above fifteen people.

▶ Four couples who live in a small Indiana town have been meeting to discuss films for three years now. They are all in their twenties and thirties, and most of them are well-educated professionals. Two of the couples now have a child, and one of these women no longer works outside the home. One person in every couple is employed by the same large company, and they began meeting because they missed the access to movies they had experienced in larger towns. They have to drive over an hour to Indianapolis, but they do it regularly, with pleasure. Occasionally, they have rented a video when the weather was bad or one of them had a sick child. (The couples with children plan for a baby-sitter far ahead.) They usually pick the last Saturday or Sunday of the month. Their routine is to drive into the city around 3 P.M., see a movie at about 4:30, and discuss it over dinner at a restaurant. The women tend to choose the movies and restaurants through phone conversations, and the men don't seem to mind. They have grown quite close through their movie group, and they dread the day that one of them will be transferred to another town. They have no interest in enlarging the group at present.

▶ There is a group in Iowa City that focuses on classic films, which they watch on videos or, recently, DVDs.

In the last few years, as we have increasingly shared our experience with the world, members of our group have been asked to consult with new groups that are forming. We usually go—alone or as a team—to the first meeting. We talk about our suggestions for process and rules, and then we usually sit back and listen. At the end, we comment on the issues we have observed and make recommendations for future meetings.

Brief descriptions of the eight groups we have helped to start are as follows:

▶ a young university alumni group;

▶ six suburban couples, mostly in their forties;

▶ a New York City group of professional women;

▶ a high-school extracurricular activity;

▶ a church-based young singles group;

▶ a community center–based group of active seniors;

▶ a loosely affiliated group of young apartment-dwellers; and

▶ a mixed-age group of extended family members.

In the group of suburban couples, it had been decided, before our involvement, that they would bring their children to one another's homes. Their kids range from six to fourteen, and the parents felt that the kids could take care of themselves in a separate room provided by each host. The older kids were paid a little bit to care for the younger ones. Our consultants were dubious about the parents' ability to concentrate, but, at least on the first night, it worked perfectly. The hosts provided food that the kids loved, as well as materials for various projects. All the parents checked on their kids after dinner, and they offered rewards for every child who did not bother the parents during discussion time. (They had seen the film previously.)

Our member who helped start the young alumni group was called "The Movie Nazi" because he insisted on turn-taking. The host that night told him that it was *her* house and she would speak whenever she wanted to. He was stymied for a moment, but the rest of the group let her have it, and the group process moved on.

The church-based singles group contained some fundamentalist Christians. These individuals discussed the movie primarily as it related to their church and the Bible, and our consultants thought it was unfortunate that the assistant pastor was a participant because he seemed to provide a dampening influence on others. Some group members also found the language and sexuality offensive in that night's movie. This is a tough one! Since openness to new experiences and the viewpoints of others, we feel, is vital to the success of a film group, we wondered aloud whether this was really the best activity for such a group. We suggested that they try three movie nights before they decide about continuing.

CHAPTER 15

OUR POWER TO CREATE
BETTER FILMS

There is no doubt that book groups have influenced the publishing industry in significant ways. Movie groups have great potential to do the same for the film industry.

IT'S SHOW *BUSINESS*

The economics of show business (emphasis on the *business* part) seem to be making it harder and harder to find good films—that is, films intellectually and emotionally satisfying to adults. There are several reasons for this:

▶ Most studios are now owned by huge, multinational corporations, and their executives' eyes are focused on profits and shareholder value. Although one might expect that smaller-budget movies would have a better chance of making profits, it is really the big-budget films that make the biggest profits. Every studio wants to make another *Titanic,* which people will see over and over. Studio bigwigs think in terms of sequels or titles that have recognizable drawing power. Executives run scared because, in the film industry, mistakes get a person fired, and the turnover is way above the corporate average. Getting anything greenlit (approved for funding) is a miracle because no individual wants to take responsibility. And getting anything unusual or out-of-the-Hollywood-formula through the studio system is almost impossible.

▶ As our economy has become more global, so, too, have the markets for movies. Indeed, more than half of the revenue for movies now comes from outside North America. Fortunately for the United States, English is becoming more universal, but all the world does not yet speak English well. Therefore, action movies are a lot more saleable than ones with complicated dialogue. Huge profits are also made on the merchandising of spin-off products, and these are unlikely to come from character-driven dramas.

▶ In contrast to many other industries, the movie business is still growing. The Motion Picture Association of America (MPAA) reports a record $9.5 billion box-office take for 2002 in this country alone. The 1.64 billion tickets sold represent a 10.2 percent increase for 2002 over 2001—the largest admissions percentage increase since 1957. The average American went to the movies 5.7 times during the year, and the average ticket price was

$5.81. Internationally, moviegoing rose 7.5 percent over the previous year, with 7.3 billion tickets sold. But the cost of making films also skyrocketed. Making and marketing the average Hollywood movie rose to $89.4 million in 2002—a 13.6 percent increase over 2001.

▶ Who goes to the movies most? According to Jack Valenti of the MPAA:

Ages 12 to 29 make up about 50 percent of the audience.

Ages 30 to 49 make up about 32%.

Ages 50 and over make up about 17%.

Young people, then, are the big moviegoers. And what do young people want? Action. Generation Xers and generation Yers were the first people totally raised with TV, video games, and computers, and their world moves very quickly. They have shorter attention spans than older people do. Generation Y teenagers, especially, like and expect technology and speed.

▶ And who chooses the movie that teens attend? Several surveys show that boys do when girls and boys go together. Any trip to the multiplex demonstrates that young people mostly go to the movies on dates or in coed groups. In these instances, testosterone seems to rule! But girls also attend movies in groups, and films like *Bring It On, Clueless,* and *Save the Last Dance* have demonstrated that there is also big box-office potential for films that appeal to teenaged and preteen girls.

▶ It is not unusual to talk about movies with a middle-aged friend and learn that he or she hasn't been to a theater for five—even ten or twenty—years. Older people give lots of reasons for not going to movies:

There aren't any good films anymore.

They are extremely busy with work, kids, and aging parents.

They find a night out too expensive with the high cost of a movie, restaurant, parking, and the babysitter.

They are too tired and would rather rent a video or DVD.

They have been burned by critics who often give high ratings only to those films that have a new and different style.

▶ Many adults are no longer sure what they want to see. Nothing is quite as clear now as it seemed a few years ago. Every issue has many angles to it. Mature people now want realistic complications. We want subtlety. We recognize angst. But we also want to be entertained, and we don't want to be depressed. It is not easy to make films that satisfy all those criteria.

▶ It is now extremely difficult to get small, independent, low-budget films made *and* picked up for distribution. Some smaller companies like Miramax used to take chances, but Disney now owns Miramax, and other conglomerates have bought up similar independent studios, so the situation is increasingly profit driven. In the eighties and nineties, independent movies seemed glamorous and lucrative, but quite a few people lost a lot of money. Smaller movies are now only financed by small companies (often going bankrupt), wealthy "angel" investors, or starving filmmakers who max out their credit cards and go into debt. And now, getting these movies picked up for distribution at film festivals or trade exhibits is increasingly rare because major distribution can cost as much as $40 million. Printing copies of films for a major rollout in theaters is very expensive, and the much-talked-about digital revolution is not happening for lots of valid reasons. Advertising, too, is increasingly expensive, but it's necessary because people don't get into theater seats unless their eyeballs have been engaged by some kind of media attention—or, more rarely, by word-of-mouth. Therefore, distributors are increasingly cautious. Similarly, big advances from foreign sales agents or video stores are a thing of the past. So the days of young, talented filmmakers shooting something for under a million and getting $10 million in a bidding war at Sundance are pretty much over.

OUR POTENTIAL

It's as simple as this: If more people belonged to movie groups, more adults would see movies. These people would be choosing the intelligent, well-made films that warrant discussion. Consequently, the movies that fit those criteria would make more money, and the powers that be would see more reason to invest in those types of films. As a result, better films would get made.

Individuals as well as groups can influence the kinds of movies that are available—with their dollars. If you care about quality films, don't go only to the blockbusters that you know are mindless. Don't allow yourself to be unduly influenced by manipulative marketing. Full-page newspaper ads and frequent TV commercials often signify desperate studios, hoping that hype will make people go to their movies without reading reviews. Executives are now able to tell by Saturday of the initial weekend—sometimes even by Friday night—how much money their film will make. The studios count on these first-weekend customers not reading reviews.

Movie trailers also can be very misleading. It is not uncommon for all of us to love a trailer, only to be extremely disappointed by the film. The trailer may show the best scenes while the rest of the film is garbage. Or the genre may be very different than it appears to be. Studio execs plan on our buying the hype and not investigating.

We consumers all make poor movie choices sometimes, but we should support the more intelligent offerings. Even at a filmmaker's forum recently—filled with current and potential film professionals—the audience was asked how many of them had seen two disappointing yet successful big films, and most of the hands went up. Then they were asked about two excellent but obscure films, and only a quarter of the hands went up. The moderator's next question was, "Do you think there is any connection between your choices and your complaining about what gets made?"

The film industry needs to find more ways of educating people about good films and better ways of getting adults back into theaters. It is a chicken-and-egg problem: adults say there's nothing worthwhile to see, and moviemakers say they can't make money on more intelligent films because people don't go to see them. Maybe the efforts of Robert Redford to create more theaters showing independent films will bear fruit in better economic times. Perhaps, if we take time to share our ideas with friends and family about good films, we will have some influence. And maybe an *explosion* in movie groups will help.

Just as book groups have kept publishers from cutting off midlist books (those that are neither on best-seller lists nor required buying for academics) and have singlehandedly kept some small, independent bookstores in business, movie groups could exert a lot of influence. Just as major publishers print readers' guides, fill their Web sites with discussion tips, and even set up conference calls between authors and book groups, so, too, might studios and producers facilitate the choices and discussions of movie groups someday.

It would be great if movie groups could have an even more powerful effect on moviemaking than book groups have on publishers! We should be writing positive letters or e-mails to studios and producers when they make an intelligent film, and we should let them know when their product stinks. In the future, we could form loose associations of movie groups, rating films for their discussibility and giving feedback to the producers. We could urge print and electronic media to think about films in the context of our criteria. A variety of movie group mavens could offer reviews that would matter to film groups—perhaps in a Web site or newsletter.

Filmmakers need to be reminded that adults have disposable income and time—often more than kids do—and adults want to see "themselves" on the screen. They want to see their own reality there. They want to be engaged by some ambiguity in the story and some maturity in the characters. If better movies are made, the adult audience will come—at least, those who are in movie groups.

FROM HERE TO ETERNITY

Part IV

(FILM INFORMATION)

CHAPTER 16

FIFTY-EIGHT FILMS: OUR
RATINGS AND DISCUSSIONS

Since our first movie group meeting in May 1996, we have seen a total of fifty-eight films. Every year we have had between eight and ten sessions.

Our highest average ratings (on a scale of one to ten) went to:

Remember the Titans (9.1)

The Pianist (8.9)

Cookie's Fortune (8.8)

Changing Lanes (8.6)

As Good As It Gets (8.6)

Secrets and Lies (8.5)

Shall We Dance? (8.5)

Sling Blade (8.5)

The Cider House Rules (8.4)

The Widow of St. Pierre (8.1)

The English Patient (8)

The lowest average ratings were for:

A.I. (4.7)
Beloved (4.9)
The Trigger Effect (5.1)

The widest ranges, indicating the most disagreement, were for:

Breaking the Waves (−1 to 9)
Memento (0 to 9)
Gladiator (1 to 9)
A.I. (1 to 9)
Antonia's Line (2 to 10)
Boys Don't Cry (1 to 8)
Being John Malkovich (3 to 10)
All About My Mother (2 to 9)
Beloved (2 to 8)
Run Lola Run (3 to 9)
Billy Elliot (4 to 10)
Monsoon Wedding (4 to 10)
Far from Heaven (3 to 9)

Our ratings of the films we have seen may be of interest to others, and the discussions that we got into may serve as examples of the subjects that a movie can lead to. Some movie groups may have to rely on videos because they live in small towns, cannot physically get to theaters, or just prefer to organize a group around videos. Some individuals may simply want to rent a good flick on a Saturday night. Thus, we would like to give you the benefit of our acquired wisdom regarding these fifty-eight films.

A quick reminder here: Any group should record their musings. We didn't at the beginning and then had to reconstruct what we could remember because we wanted a record.

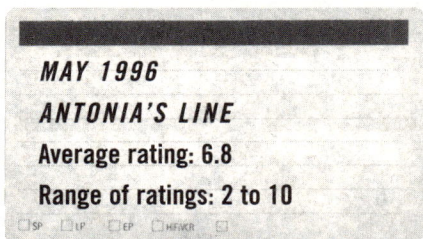

MAY 1996
ANTONIA'S LINE
Average rating: 6.8
Range of ratings: 2 to 10

☐SP ☐LP ☐EP ☐HF/VCR ☐

This film, in Dutch with English subtitles, was written and directed by Marleen Gorris. It won the Academy Award for best foreign film in 1995. It portrays the lives of three generations of strong, independent Dutch women but is especially focused on the matriarch, Antonia. She leaves her village before World War II and later returns with her artist daughter, finding a place for herself by supporting underdogs against cruel villagers and celebrating all kinds of quirky, unconventional love. Our group differed on the use of violence, including rape and murder. Most felt it was integral to the story, but some were offended by seemingly gratuitous scenes. Some people found the film depressing, but two women were inspired by the resilience of the women and the relationships in the film. Many loved the scenery and cinematography, and most found the film to be hopeful—even beautiful. We talked a bit about strong women, but, since this was our first meeting, we segued right into the rules (which had been made by three women).

JUNE 1996
COLD COMFORT FARM
Average rating: 6.3
Range of ratings: 4 to 8
☐ SP ☐ LP ☐ EP ☐ HF/VCR ☐

John Schlesinger directed this film, starring Eileen Atkins, Kate Beckinsale, and Ian McKellen. It is set in England in the early 1930s. The Beckinsale character, Flora Poste, has been recently orphaned, with only a small income, and she is sent to live with distant relatives on a farm. Flora is determined to sort everything out. Some of our male members were put off by the slow, Jane Austen–type style, and some of us had difficulty understanding the dialogue. Several people loved the pluckiness of the young, cheerful Flora as she deals with the depravity of the farm people. In general, the characters were seen as well cast and very well acted. Some of us, however, said the story seemed dated. There was some talk about farm living, and we learned that three of our members grew up on farms. Sympathy was expressed for orphaned children, which prompted the disclosure that one of our members was adopted. Two of us have adopted children.

SEPTEMBER 1996
THE TRIGGER EFFECT
Average rating: 5.1
Range of ratings: 3 to 7
☐ SP ☐ LP ☐ EP ☐ HF/VCR ☐

Written and directed by David Koepp, this films stars Kyle MacLachlan, Elisabeth Shue, and Dermot Mulroney. The theme is man's tenuous hold on civility when survival is at stake. When the electricity goes off for several days in a suburban town, a young couple finds out how predatory human nature is. The issues include: rivalries among friends; finding medicine for a sick baby; discovering a looting stranger; and a scary incident when people are trying to siphon gas. We found the premise and setup very interesting but the story development inadequate. The ending is sentimental and unsatisfying. Nevertheless, we thought that the feelings this film provoked in us were worth examining. Would we do violent things in this situation? Most thought we would do anything to protect ourselves and our children. Is this scenario likely in our day and age? We were split between those who said no and others who came up with all kinds of doomsday possibilities.

OCTOBER 1996
SECRETS AND LIES
Average rating: 8.5
Range of ratings: 6 to 9.5
☐ SP ☐ LP ☐ EP ☐ HPWR ☐

This is a British film, written and directed by Mike Leigh. We loved Brenda Blethyn as the mother who gave up her child for adoption at birth and Marianne Jean-Baptiste as the successful, adult daughter who searches for her birth mother. When they meet, the shock that the daughter is black while the mother is white is a priceless moment. The mother lives a lower-class life in London with her difficult, sassy daughter and her upwardly mobile photographer brother. She is lonely but not at all ready for this reunion, and she tries to deny the facts. As the secrets and truths unfold, the process of bringing warmth to the whole family is masterful. Our only complaint was missing some "pearl" lines because of the British accents. We moved easily into a discussion of adoption. Of those among us who have adopted, one person knows the birth parents and their history; the other couple knows nothing. We talked at length about open versus closed adoptions. None of us thought it would be easy if a child suddenly contacted us, as in this film, but about half said that any parent-child connection is a good thing.

NOVEMBER 1996
THE ENGLISH PATIENT
Average rating: 8
Range of ratings: 5 to 10

Directed by Anthony Minghella from the novel by Michael Ondaatje, this film has a stellar cast: Ralph Fiennes, Kristin Scott Thomas, Juliette Binoche, and Willem Dafoe. Much of the story is told in flashbacks, but it begins in the 1930s when a Hungarian mapmaker joins several British explorers in the Sahara Desert. He falls madly in love, but the couple is shot down in a plane crash. He tries to get help, experiencing betrayal along the way, and is then almost killed in a fiery plane crash. In the final days of World War II, he is taken to a villa in Italy where a young shell-shocked nurse cares for him and hears his story. This is an exceptional and complex movie—both in story and emotions. Several of us saw it twice. Many noted the breathtaking cinematography. We learned that we have at least one World War II history buff among us, and he filled in some of the facts. We also talked about the nurse's actions with her dying patient—whether they were right or wrong. Could or would we do the same thing?

JANUARY 1997

SHINE

Average rating: 7.8

Range of ratings: 6 to 9

☐ SP ☐ LP ☐ EP ☐ HI/FI/VCR ☐

This Australian film is based on the life story of David Helf-gott, the concert pianist who was driven hard by his father and teachers and had a mental breakdown. It stars Geoffrey Rush, with Lynn Redgrave as the woman who helps him survive and thrive. It is cowritten and directed by Scott Hicks. The story, told largely in flashbacks, is very moving. David is a talented child prodigy, but he and his siblings are abused by their father, who himself was the victim of European atrocities. David breaks away and achieves success but, after the breakdown, ends up in a mental institution. Many years later, he plays the piano in a bar, but, through several twists and the love of a good woman, he returns to the concert hall and to happiness. We loved the acting and the story as well as the incredibly beautiful music. Some felt that Rush's antics were a bit over the top at times, and a few found the recovery implausible. Our discussion focused on mental illness and institutions, and, coincidentally, we had a psychiatrist guest that night who thought that the film was pretty realistic. We also learned that two of our members are pianists, and one had had a short concert career.

FEBRUARY 1997
BREAKING THE WAVES
Average rating: 5.8
Range of ratings: –1 to 9
SP   LP   EP   HI/WOX

Written and directed by Lars von Trier, the film stars Emily Watson and Stellan Skarsgård. It is a drama set in a deeply religious, repressed area of Northern Scotland, and the role of religion is prominent throughout. A young, naïve woman falls in love with a powerful Danish oil-rig worker. He is paralyzed in an accident on the rig and cannot perform sexually when he returns to her. However, he insists that she find other lovers and describe it all to him. She becomes more and more deviant, always believing that she is guided by God. Her degradation and humiliation are heartbreaking, and the ending will stay in your mind a long time. The average rating for this film was pulled down by four people who absolutely hated the graphic violence, sexuality, and nudity. Others loved the powerful portrayals of interesting characters. Two of us considered this a remarkable film with flawless performances. The role of religion in the story was discussed, with the dissenters feeling that this was no excuse for her actions. Most of the women blamed the man for pushing a vulnerable girl, but most of the men thought that she had the responsibility for her actions.

MARCH 1997

SLING BLADE

Average rating: 8.5

Range of ratings: 6 to 10

☐ SP   ☐ LP   ☐ EP   ☐ HiFi/VCR   ☐

Billy Bob Thornton is the writer, director, and star of this unusual film. Other actors include Dwight Yoakam, John Ritter, and Robert Duvall. It has an un-Hollywood-like plot about a retarded man who was hospitalized at age twelve after killing his mother and her boyfriend. Now an adult, he is released to start a new life in the small town where he had lived. He gets a job fixing motors and befriends a young boy and his mother, tentatively finding a place for himself. Everything seems hopeful until violence occurs between the mother and her boyfriend. Most of us loved this film. The characters appear to be simple, but they gradually reveal complex emotions. Even the damaged man can be a hero. The limited action is beautifully paced, and the acting is magnificent. The whole movie seems very real. Only a couple of us found the film slow and ponderous. Some people saw no excuse for murder. Our discussion was first about the mentally handicapped. Two members of the group have severe retardation in their family, and they gave us some feel for institutionalization versus home care. We also talked about the moral dilemma of murder to stop a violent situation, and most of us thought that any normal person must find another way.

APRIL 1997

KOLYA

Average rating: 8.1

Range of ratings: 7 to 9.5

☐ SP ☐ LP ☐ EP ☐ HF/VCR ☐

This movie won the Academy Award for best foreign film of 1996. The language is Czech and Russian. It was directed by Jan Sverák. Zdenek Sverák is the writer and star. He plays Kolya, a concert cellist who was kicked out of the state orchestra and must make his living by performing at funerals and painting tombstones. A lifelong bachelor with debts to pay, he agrees when his friend suggests marrying a Russian woman for money so that she can leave Russia. She then runs to her lover in West Germany, leaving her five-year-old son with his grandmother. However, the grandmother dies, and the boy is sent to Kolya, his stepfather. The ending is predictable but lovely. The boy, a terrific actor, weaves his magic, and Kolya gradually falls in love with him. Our only negative comments were that this is a "small" story and a bit slow at times. Overall, it is a beautiful film and very worthwhile. Most of us described situations wherein we started out disliking a person but were turned around by some circumstance. The women, and some of the men, could not abide anyone being cruel to a child.

SEPTEMBER 1997

MASK CLASS

☐ SP ☐ LP ☐ EP ☐ HF/VCR ☐

A diversion from the model! One of our members is on the board of a locally renowned theater group, and he invited the director to do a workshop on masks. Our guest, a university teacher as well as a very animated director and actor, educated us about many aspects of masks—why different countries produce different types; how they are used in training actors; and how we use psychological masks in everyday life. We liked the experimentation with a different model, but we felt vaguely dissatisfied at the end of the evening. It didn't take long to determine why! We had been more listeners than participants, and the group camaraderie had been interrupted. We had had a stranger in our midst, and he was in an unusual role.

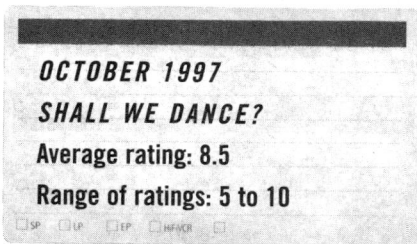

OCTOBER 1997
SHALL WE DANCE?
Average rating: 8.5
Range of ratings: 5 to 10
☐ SP ☐ LP ☐ EP ☐ HI-FI/VCR ☐

This is a Japanese comedy with English subtitles. The writer-director is Masayuki Suo. The main character is an ordinary Japanese accountant. He has a middle-class life with a doting wife and daughter, but he is not happy. One day he sees a beautiful young woman in a dancing academy, and he signs up for lessons. Even though he is ashamed of his poor skills, he perseveres in both dancing and longing for the young girl. He hides all this from his coworkers and family, all of which is shown in hysterically funny scenes that give the viewer insights about Japanese life. The theme is really not about dancing, however. It is about learning who we are and having the courage to go after what we want. But the dancing is beautiful, too, and the music is uplifting. Some of us disliked the silliness and the big, predictable dance contest finale, but most of us loved the warmth of the message and the use of dance as a metaphor. Most called this a unique and beautiful film. Our discussion focused on the differences between middle managers in Japan and the United States. Three of our group have had business experience in Japan, and none of them would want to trade places. As to the message about finding your passion, there was some cynicism. Few of us have done things so out of character as this, but some said they'd like to.

NOVEMBER 1997
THE WINGS OF THE DOVE
Average rating: 6.5
Range of ratings: 4 to 9
☐ SP ☐ LP ☐ EP ☐ HF/VCR ☐

This drama, set in the early 1900s, is based on the Henry James novel. It was directed by Iain Softley, and its stars include Helena Bonham Carter and Charlotte Rampling. The main character is an impoverished young Englishwoman. Her mother threw away her own wealth for the love of a worthless man and is determined that her daughter not do the same. So the young woman temporarily rejects her lover and goes to Venice with her aunt. She meets an incredibly rich young American woman there, who is later attracted to the Englishwoman's boyfriend. When Bonham Carter's character learns that the American is dying, she forges a plan for her boyfriend to receive the money. The twists and turns of the plot are sometimes passionate, sometimes very dark, and always multilayered. We liked the acting, especially Helena Bonham Carter, and we enjoyed the beautiful costumes and scenery, but we found the details of the plot dated and somewhat difficult to relate to. We noted how different class and money are today. A lively discussion ensued about how the genders still operate differently in order to get money, and we talked about what it takes for either men or women to marry for money.

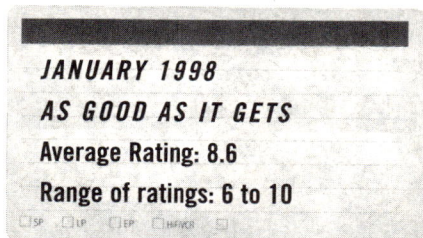

JANUARY 1998
AS GOOD AS IT GETS
Average Rating: 8.6
Range of ratings: 6 to 10
☐SP ☐LP ☐EP ☐HI/FM/CR ☐

This comedy was one of our all-time favorites. Our opinions can be found in chapter 4, which details an audio recording of our interaction.

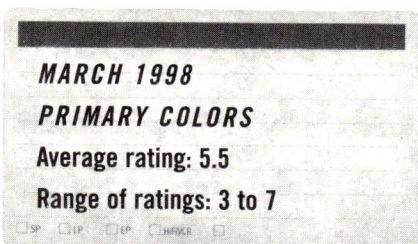

MARCH 1998
PRIMARY COLORS
Average rating: 5.5
Range of ratings: 3 to 7
☐SP ☐LP ☐EP ☐HI/FM/CR ☐

This film is based on the infamous Joe Klein (originally "Anonymous") novel. Mike Nichols directed, and Elaine May wrote the screenplay. The big-name cast includes John Travolta, Emma Thompson, Billy Bob Thornton, Kathy Bates, Larry Hagman, and Rob Reiner. The Travolta character, clearly based on Bill Clinton, is running for president. He has incredible political skills but can't keep his pants on long enough to stay out of trouble, and he has a large appetite for food, too. His young aide must deal with crises that are both funny and sad. This is an entertaining and biting satire about the political process, but, with all the talent invested in this project, we expected more—more laughs and more insights. We agreed that it is hard for actors to impersonate characters who are still on the world stage, and we wondered whether this project should have been made a few years later. In general, we were amused to find that the Democrats among us rated it highly and defended Clinton quite strongly, while the Republicans among us felt "dirty" about the whole thing. We speculated about what parts of the story are true. We shared a few laughs about politics but agreed that this is a very dark comedy.

APRIL 1998
THE SPANISH PRISONER
Average rating: 5.6
Range of ratings: 4 to 8
☐ SP ☐ LP ☐ EP ☐ HIFI VCR ☐

This thriller was written and directed by David Mamet. It stars Ben Gazzara, Steve Martin, and Campbell Scott. A young man, who has designed a profitable process for his company, seeks help from a wealthy stranger to ensure that he gets credit and payment. When this stranger is shown to be dangerous, the young man looks to the FBI for help, and the FBI arranges a sting. But suddenly, this young man is not only conned but also framed for murder. We found this movie confusing and somehow "off." The dialogue is smart but weird. The pacing is slow at first, then frenetic and wild. The acting is fine, but the direction leaves a lot to be desired. Some felt that all of this is typical Mamet, but others expected better from him. Those who generally like mysteries had fun trying to figure it all out, but many found the film frustrating, and most of us thought the ending was weak. We had some discussion about why only some people like mysteries. Then we got into a heavy conversation about which partner in a couple chooses the movie, and we found that men and women each choose about half the time. Most couples consult each other, but one person usually takes the lead. Some insist on previewing before they choose for the group, although nobody really wants to get into that habit.

MAY 1998
THE HORSE WHISPERER
Average rating: 7.2
Range of ratings: 4 to 10
☐ SP ☐ LP ☐ EP ☐ HiFi/VCR ☐

Robert Redford directed and stars in this drama. The cast also includes Kristin Scott Thomas, Sam Neill, Dianne Wiest, and Scarlett Johansson, who does a marvelous job as a wounded teenager. In a graphic, powerful scene at the beginning, the girl and her horse are hit by a truck, and both of them are badly injured. The girl's psychological injuries are especially worrisome to her high-powered mother, so the mother finds a horse healer in Montana. The horse whisperer reluctantly accepts the challenge and proceeds to work his magic on both the girl and the horse. He and the mother also fall in love, and they both must decide between her marriage and their passion. Some of us loved this storyline and the tender intensity of these relationships. Others found the story trite and unbelievable. The three members who had read the book agreed that the film is better—particularly the ending. Many of us commented on the wonderful cinematography and the gorgeous Montana sunsets. We all agreed that there are credibility issues such as the hauling across country of an injured horse by two incompetent females. This film sparked an interesting discussion about fast-track, high-pressure, frequently East Coast lives versus more laid-back Western ones, and we were divided on whether this difference is a myth or a reality. Figuring out what we want in life is not easy. We talked a lot about whether the mother and father would stay together in the end and whether the mother and the cowboy could have been happy together (the consensus on the latter issue was no).

SEPTEMBER 1998
YOUR FRIENDS & NEIGHBORS
Average rating: 5.7
Range of ratings: 3 to 8

Written and directed by Neil LaBute, the cast members are Amy Brenneman, Aaron Eckhart, Catherine Keener, Nastassja Kinski, Jason Patric, and Ben Stiller. This is truly an ensemble piece. One husband and another man's wife have an affair, and that causes a series of repercussions in other relationships. The characters seem obsessed with sex, and they are all very self-involved. There is little story here, but there is a lot about behavior and conflict. Our group, in general, found the dialogue interesting, albeit terribly disturbing at times. We agreed that this movie about sex is not very sexy. Many people said that they could not relate to any of these characters, and someone said that she wanted to slap them all. A few of us were sympathetic to these young people trying to find their way in the world, but most of us found them shallow and annoying. The blatant sex and crude language offended two members. We talked about our pleasure when a character got his or her comeuppance and applied that to situations in our own lives. We agreed that some scenes were creative and clever and that the film has a strange power.

OCTOBER 1998
PLEASANTVILLE
Average rating: 7.3
Range of ratings: 6 to 8
☐ SP ☐ LP ☐ EP ☐ HF/VCR ☐

This fantasy-comedy was written and directed by Gary Ross. It stars Tobey Maguire, Reese Witherspoon, Jeff Daniels, Joan Allen, and William H. Macy. Two teenaged siblings, bored with life, watch a 1950s TV sitcom about a small town, and they suddenly find themselves whisked away to a black and white, simple, pleasant place. Their clothes and parents are different from their previous ones. Both kids want to get out, but the boy tries to fit in while the girl rebels. The old-fashioned values and the levels of innocence and naïveté are shocking to behold from our modern perspective. However, as the girl flaunts rules, color appears. The two kids help their mother break out of her pleasant cage, but they also begin to enjoy some of the 1950s values. Overall, this is a good fairy tale, with provocative issues of conservatism and liberalism. We were all blown away by the innovative use of color. Most of us neither loved nor hated the film, finding it interesting but fairly forgettable. Some of us found the characters too one-dimensional—unrealistic even for the fifties. Nevertheless, the film provoked a good discussion about values and the fact that there seem to be good and bad ones in every generation.

NOVEMBER 1998
BELOVED
Overall rating: 4.9
Range of ratings: 2 to 8

Jonathan Demme directed this drama, based on the prize-winning book by Toni Morrison. The cast includes Oprah Winfrey and Danny Glover. Sometime after the Civil War, a former slave lives proudly in Ohio with her daughter. Another former slave finds them and moves in to help run the farm and perhaps renew their romance. Suddenly the house shakes violently and a young girl appears. She behaves strangely and affects all of those around her in powerful ways. The past is explored, and we learn that this is the spirit of the slave woman's dead daughter. After so much hype and anticipation for this film, our group was uniformly disappointed. Those who had read the book explained why the story is so confusing. We praised the acting and thought Oprah was phenomenal. We appreciated getting a new slant on post-slavery times. But many of us found the fantasy girl and her antics off-putting. We would like to have seen the love story developed more. The film was too long, and the whole thing seemed overwrought. Nevertheless, we felt that we had learned a few things.

JANUARY 1999
A CIVIL ACTION
Average rating: 6.1
Range of ratings: 5 to 7

Steve Zaillian, who won an Oscar for writing *Schindler's List*, wrote and directed this drama-thriller. John Travolta is effective as a lawyer on an environmental crusade, and Robert Duvall gives an outstanding performance. For our group, the ratings range was unusually narrow. We agreed that the script was weak and that there were no characters one really cared about. It seems that the victims are given short shrift. The fate of the lawyers is more important than the people who were harmed. Nevertheless, the dynamic performances and courtroom antics made it worthwhile, and we got into a long analysis of the United States legal system. The one attorney in our group bore the brunt of our rants quite bravely!

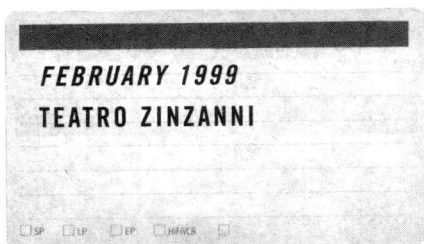

FEBRUARY 1999
TEATRO ZINZANNI

☐ SP ☐ LP ☐ EP ☐ HFI/VCR ☐

We attended a performance of this West Coast comedy troupe. They have a huge, ornate European tent, and the event is a unique experience. The evening includes a gourmet dinner as well as singers, musicians, mimes, clowns, and other circus performers. We enjoyed this rather mindless entertainment and agreed on a rating of 9 for its genre.

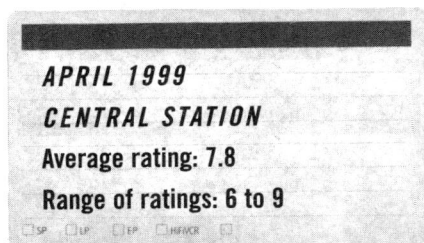

APRIL 1999
CENTRAL STATION
Average rating: 7.8
Range of ratings: 6 to 9

☐ SP ☐ LP ☐ EP ☐ HFI/VCR ☐

This Brazilian (with subtitles) road movie stars Fernanda Montenegro as a cynical older woman, who is badgered into helping a young boy find his father. As they travel about the countryside, many tragicomic incidents help them to form a bond. The woman changes before our eyes as the boy works his way into her heart. Montenegro was nominated for the best actress Oscar, and the film was in the running for best foreign language movie. Our group loved Montenegro's shaded and complex performance and thought she should have won (instead of Gwyneth Paltrow for *Shakespeare in Love*). We talked about how one person can change another's life and how random events can have the most powerful impacts. We related chance events from our own or friends' lives that have affected us. There was also a lengthy discussion about how we deal with beggars, especially children, when we encounter them in crowded urban centers.

MAY 1999
COOKIE'S FORTUNE
Average rating: 8.8
Range of ratings: 7 to 9.25

This was a highly anticipated Robert Altman film, and it did not disappoint us. Patricia Neal stars as an eccentric Mississippi widow nicknamed Cookie. Glenn Close is her domineering niece, Julianne Moore is a ditzy niece, Liv Tyler is a rebellious young woman, and Charles Dutton is Cookie's wonderful caretaker. The film has an authentic Southern feel. The characters are really characters, and there are many laugh-out-loud scenes. We thought it was a little slow at first, but the plot really kicks in when Cookie is murdered and the whole town is turned upside down. The dysfunctionality of this family and their greed for Cookie's money are themes we could all relate to. Indeed, we talked a long time about family relationships where money is involved versus the benefits when there is no money to inherit.

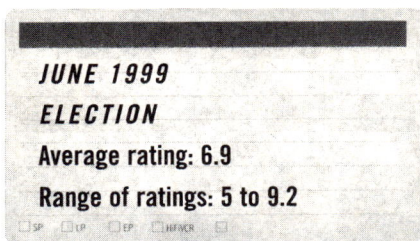

JUNE 1999
ELECTION
Average rating: 6.9
Range of ratings: 5 to 9.2

☐ SP   ☐ LP   ☐ EP   ☐ HIFI/VCR   ☐

This is a comedy seemingly about high school politics but really about relationships and choices in life. Reese Witherspoon is an ambitious senior who schemes and cheats her way into student body leadership positions; Matthew Broderick plays a young teacher trying to block her path. He almost succeeds, but she turns the tables on him, and the ending is very provocative. There was a lot of dissension in our group about this film. All the characters are flawed, but all are recognizable. Most of us loved the acting and laughed a lot, but three people hated seeing a bad person win, and one man saw nothing in this young woman to admire. Some people were sure that she would get her comeuppance later in life, while others thought that she would continue to have great success. We talked about high school—how it was for us and how it is for our kids. And we talked at great length about what it takes to succeed in life—the tradeoffs that some people are willing to make, and how we individually define success.

JULY 1999
RUN LOLA RUN
Average rating: 6.7
Range of ratings: 3 to 9
☐SP ☐LP ☐EP ☐HF-VCR ☐

This German thriller, written and directed by Tom Tykwer, has English subtitles. The young woman star is Franka Potente, and her boyfriend is played by Moritz Bleibtreu. It presents three consecutive versions of a story in which the girl is trying to save her boyfriend from vicious gangsters. This device is innovative, and the idea that random events can have a major effect on outcomes is interesting. But our group was widely split on this film. Those who loved it talked of the constant action and great, pounding music. They related to acts of kindness and positive thoughts that can help bring good outcomes. Those who hated it found it slow, with no acting challenges. They could not relate to the characters, and they thought the running, running was boring, boring. This film provoked an interesting discussion about luck versus chance. Some members consider themselves very lucky, while others do not believe in such a thing. There was agreement that, although there are some truly random events in our lives, we ourselves create most of what we call luck.

AUGUST 1999
THE DINNER GAME
Average rating: 7.9
Range of ratings: 5 to 9
☐SP ☐LP ☐EP ☐HF-VCR ☐

This is a French (subtitled) comedy directed by Francis Veber. It stars Theirry Lhermitte as a mean-spirited bon vivant and Jacques Villeret as the idiot he means to humiliate at a dinner party. This is a game that a group of friends cooked up in which each member takes his turn by inviting someone they can all make fun of. As we get to know both characters better, we find that the bon vivant has been jilted by his wife. She had good reasons; he lacks any facility for introspection. The more limited man, however, is honest and appealing. In the end, he plays the game well, and the tables are turned. Only two of us were negative about this film. To those two, the story is upsetting and politically incorrect. The rest of us thought this film is superb. We laughed out loud. The idiot is a real man, and the evil person gets what he deserves. Our group then picked up on the theme of marriage. The marriage in this film is clearly not a friendship, and there is nothing more important than that ingredient. One woman introduced her criteria for attractive qualities in a mate, and she got agreement that honesty is at the top of the list. Both genders said that looks are less and less important as we age, but the women seemed more sure of this than the men were.

OCTOBER 1999
AMERICAN BEAUTY
Average rating: 7.8
Range of ratings: 6 to 9

☐ SP   ☐ LP   ☐ EP   ☐ HF/VCR   ☐

Sam Mendes, who previously worked in theater, directed this interesting movie. Kevin Spacey stars as a fed-up husband and father having a midlife crisis, and Annette Bening is his successful, driven, uptight wife. Three wild and crazy adolescents are played by Thora Birch, Mena Suvari, and Wes Bentley. We judged this to be an innovative and beautifully realized film. Although midlife crises are hardly new, there are some twists to Spacey's adolescent antics that are unforgettable. The director's use of rose petals is colorful and provocative. The story is played for satire as well as sadness. Those of us who loved it mentioned the casting, acting, directing, and cinematography. We thought the characters were much like people we know, albeit exaggerated, and some of us could empathize easily with them. But others thought that those exaggerations made the film trite and clichéd. The families were too dysfunctional, and the language was too crude. Most of us were bothered by Spacey's willingness to have sex with the young girl, but we were divided on whether she was telling the truth about her past. Most of the women also said that they are sick of the focus in so many movies on men's midlife crises. Our discussion did include a lot of laughs, as well as some honest exploration of midlife issues.

NOVEMBER 1999
BEING JOHN MALKOVICH
Average rating: 6.4
Range of ratings: 3 to 10
□ SP   □ LF   □ EF   □ HFWCR   □

This is an unusual film from director Spike Jonze. It stars John Cusack, John Malkovich, Cameron Diaz, and Catherine Keener. A young, down-and-out puppeteer accidentally discovers that he can invade the mind of a famous actor (Malkovich) for fifteen minutes at a time. His adventures, and those of his friends, constitute one of the most far-out stories ever presented on screen, and our group was deeply split. Two people said it is a perfect movie, with a very clever plot. Most of us thought that the acting is first-rate, and some said that they usually like the fun ride of having no idea where a movie is taking them. But the majority called it weird and bizarre. It was so far-fetched for most of us that we couldn't get into it or relate to the characters. One man added that he had learned nothing about life. Everyone thought that it would be a great violation to have one's brain invaded. It would be a form of rape. We could only relate to the story by conjuring up times when we had felt brainwashed or forced to believe something we knew was not valid.

NEW YEAR'S EVE 1999
THE CIDER HOUSE RULES
Average rating: 8.4
Range of ratings: 5 to 10
☐ SP ☐ LP ☐ EP ☐ HF/VCR ☐

Director Lasse Hallström based this film on John Irving's book and screenplay. It stars Michael Caine and Tobey Maguire. The initial setting is a World War II–era New England orphanage, which also quietly accommodates abortions. The doctor in charge has taken a young man under his wing and is encouraging the orphan to take his place medically as well as to be his surrogate son, but the young man chafes at his confinement and goes off to seek his fortune as a hired hand on the family farm of a woman who had had an abortion at the orphanage. He must prove himself both to the hardened workers and to her. Having learned some hard lessons, he eventually returns to the institution and establishes a more mature relationship with the doctor. The abortion issues were hard for one person in our group to cope with. Three reviewers were negative about the disjointed locations, saying that it felt like two different movies. A few people thought it lost energy at the end. But most of us loved the story and adored Caine's subtle, layered performance. The ambiance and antics at the orphanage were quite moving, and we felt that we had learned about a different world. This is a movie about lonely people finding love wherever they can and learning about the perils of possession. Those who had read and loved the book liked the movie even better. Despite some sadness and our tears at the ending, most of us found the film uplifting.

JANUARY 2000
THE TALENTED MR. RIPLEY
Average rating: 7.1
Range of ratings: 6 to 9

Anthony Minghella wrote and directed this version of Patricia Highsmith's novel. The stars are Matt Damon, Jude Law, and Gwyneth Paltrow. The title character, a well-educated middle-class lad, gets a trip to Rome to keep an eye on a playboy in the 1930s. He learns quickly how to dress well and live the good life, but that life gets decadent and scary at times. There is male-female as well as male-male romance and intrigue. Most of us praised the acting and the beautiful European locations. It grabbed our attention because we couldn't predict what would happen next. On the other hand, three people felt that it is slow, weird, and unbelievable. The ending is inconclusive and disappointing. We were divided on whether the bad guy would be caught. We also talked about kids and how frightening it is that we do not choose our children. We wondered what we would do if these young people were our offspring. Someone mentioned the "basements in all of us," and that provoked a discussion of how low people can go. We talked about negative surprises some of us have had regarding the values of friends and family members.

MARCH 2000
BOYS DON'T CRY
Average rating: 5.6
Range of ratings: 1 to 8

☐ SP ☐ LP ☐ EP ☐ HI-FI/CR ☐

Kimberly Peirce is the writer and director who fought hard to get this low-budget picture made. It contains a much-talked-about performance by Hilary Swank, who later won an Academy Award as best actress. Chloe Sevigny was nominated for her supporting role. It is based on the true story of Teena Brandon, who passed as a man, became romantically involved with a woman, and was eventually killed in a violent act. The range of our ratings made for a loud and stimulating discussion. The homosexuality and the selfishness of these characters surely brought out the diversity among us. On the positive side, many people said that they got sucked in by the passion and the wonderful acting. It is good for us to see disturbing films, especially when the characters elicit our compassion as these did. But the negative views were very strong, and some of us were repulsed by the violence, especially the brutal rape scene. We know these things go on, but we don't care to see them in such graphic detail. One man said that Hollyweird has now lowered the bar. After we all calmed down a bit, a discussion ensued about what our group purpose is. We have all loved being

exposed to films that we might not otherwise see and, more important, have had to think about subjects we might not otherwise consider. Our diversity is part of our strength, and there was no doubt
in anyone's mind that we have grown both as individuals and as a
group.

APRIL 2000
ALL ABOUT MY MOTHER
Average rating: 5.6
Range of ratings: 2 to 9

☐ SP ☐ LP ☐ EP ☐ HiFi/VCR ☐

This comedy-drama from Pedro
Almodóvar is in Spanish, with
English subtitles. It won both
a Golden Globe and an Acad-
emy Award for best foreign film. It focuses on a troubled woman
whose life is changed when her beloved son is run over by a car. She
encounters a series of strange people—some exploitative, some
loving, and all testing her in some way. Again, we were very widely
split in our reactions. On the positive side, one woman said that the
film teaches that love can be found in all kinds of ways and people.
Some liked the theme of sisterhood and the special support among
women. Some praised the writing and acting and said that the interesting characters kept them involved. However, several people felt
that this film is dismal and confusing. There were no messages or
insights. There were holes in the story, and several members found
it depressing. The discussion centered on how hard it is for many
of us to dwell on negative feelings. The loss of a child is especially
frightening—difficult to watch when it happens to others and
almost impossible to contemplate in one's own family.

MAY 2000

GLADIATOR

Average rating: 5.3

Range of ratings: 1 to 9

Ridley Scott directed this picture, starring Russell Crowe and Joaquin Phoenix. It is a Roman epic about a general who is captured and must become a gladiator. If he is ever to win his freedom, he must defeat both animals and men in the most brutal surroundings. Meanwhile, the politics in the ruling classes are equally brutal and deadly. This is not the kind of Hollywood blockbuster that our group usually chooses, and our first order of business was to discuss the pros and cons of the choice. Then we discovered, as suspected, that the ratings were somewhat along gender lines. Among the positives were: great acting and cinematography; a nice blending of reality and special effects; powerful action scenes and character development; and a wonderful way to learn more about history. But the negatives included: too much gratuitous violence; history lessons that are often wrong; the need for more closure in the story; and the fact that it left some of us depressed about man's inhumanity to man. There were lots of innuendoes about Russell Crowe and his sex appeal or lack of it. In general, we appreciated this diversion from our usual movie track, and one man said he was happy to see something other than weird people and kinky sex.

JULY 2000
THE PERFECT STORM
Average rating: 5.8
Range of ratings: 4 to 8
☐ SP ☐ LP ☐ EP ☐ HiFi/VCR ☐

This movie was chosen partly for the timing because we were on one couple's boat for the Fourth of July, and the irony added humor to our evaluation. The film is a costly special-effects extravaganza from director Wolfgang Petersen; the stars include George Clooney, Mark Wahlberg, and Diane Lane. It is based on the true story of a group of Massachusetts fishermen, who got caught in the most disastrous storm imaginable at sea. The setup scenes show the love interests and the backgrounds from which the men came, but the film really changes gears when the boat starts to rock and roll. No one loved this movie, and no one hated it. Most of us enjoyed it for the pure entertainment value. The special effects are phenomenal, and the storm seems to last forever—too long for some of us. George Clooney does a great job as the captain. However, some of us found the film boring because there is little character development, the men seem stupid, and the storm scenes are clearly not real. We talked at some length about the male relationships, interesting for their competition and aggression as well as their cooperation, bonding, and sacrifice. Our group also told some war stories about harrowing experiences we have had in various kinds of watercraft.

SEPTEMBER 2000

HUMAN RESOURCES

Average rating: 6.3

Range of ratings: 3 to 8

☐ SP ☐ LP ☐ EP ☐ HFR/VCR ☐

This subtitled French drama is from writer-director Laurent Cantet. A young, gung-ho college graduate returns to his family and hometown. He gets a management job in the factory where his father and many friends have worked for a lifetime. The workers exist in substandard conditions, but the management politics are intense, and the young man is caught between the two factions. Many of our group members work or have worked in human resources departments, and all of us have had dealings with HR. We found this film very thought provoking. We initially agreed with the member who said that French labor-management relations must be twenty-five years behind ours, but then we acknowledged the fact that few of us have been in small-town plants lately, and we suspect that this country still has primitive situations. We liked the warmth in this family and felt that the mother was particularly wonderful. But some of us didn't like the ending and wished there had been *some* winners. We also saw a strong union slant in the film and wished that it had been more evenhanded. This, of course, led us into conservative versus liberal politics and the value of unions. It also was a good platform for sharing some of our working experiences, and we all learned new things about one another.

OCTOBER 2000
ALMOST FAMOUS
Average rating: 7.1
Range of ratings: 5 to 10

☐ SP   ☐ LP   ☐ EP   ☐ HI/VCR   ☐

Cameron Crowe wrote and directed this attempt to capture a pivotal moment in rock and roll history. Based on Crowe's experience as a fifteen-year-old boy, the film stars Patrick Fugit as the teenager, Frances McDormand as his mother, Kate Hudson as the groupie love interest, Billy Crudup as a musician, and Philip Seymour Hoffman as a critic. The story follows the young man as he gets a writing job to travel with a band, during which he learns many of life's most difficult lessons. Most of us thought this was great entertainment. We loved the music, which took us back to our younger selves in the seventies. The characters are well developed, and we considered McDormand's performance a masterpiece. Some of us, however, were turned off by the questionable values of the characters and the prolific drug use. Two members said they felt depressed and vaguely flat when the film was over. There was some discussion about the extent to which we individually relate to rock music, which segued into what some of us were doing in the seventies. There was also some talk about how many of us would allow our child to go off as this kid did at fifteen (only one person would), as well as other challenges we have had with our kids. None of the women could imagine herself as a band groupie, but all the women could fantasize about Billy Crudup!

NOVEMBER 2000
BILLY ELLIOT
Average rating: 7.8
Range of ratings: 4 to 10
☐ SP ☐ LP ☐ EP ☐ HF/VCR ☐

This is a British tale of a miner's son (Jamie Bell), an eleven-year-old who wants to become a dancer. The difficult and unsympathetic role of his teacher is played well by Julie Walters. It is a rags-to-riches story of an awkward, misfit youngster, who finds his passion in ballet. It is not easy for his lower-class father to support him in this mining town, but family members and friends come around. The boy's relationship with his teacher runs the gamut of feelings, but there is a triumphant moment at the end. The positives for us were: the exposure to the culture of blue-collar England; the strong messages that we all should follow our dreams and be ourselves; the pure joy of dancing—both doing it and watching; and the arcs of these very interesting characters, especially the father. A couple of people thought that the film is too slow at the beginning. Some thought there are so many inconsistencies that it didn't seem real. One man hated this rude kid who didn't know how to say thanks. In the general discussion, we soon learned which members among us were dancers because they enjoyed the film so much and phrased their comments so insightfully. Some of the men related to how hard it would be to have a son like this one, and we all agreed that our children are often not who we would choose.

DECEMBER 2000
REMEMBER THE TITANS
Average rating: 9.1
Range of ratings: 8.5 to 9.9

Jerry Bruckheimer produced this sentimental story of the first football team for a newly integrated Virginia high school. Denzel Washington is the star, and Will Patton is among the other actors. Against tremendous odds both within and outside of the team, this phenomenal coach makes a motley crew into a group that can win. They not only learn to deal with racial issues and to care about one another, but they learn to make touchdowns. Some of our women had dreaded seeing a sports movie, but this one works as both a *Rocky*-style competition tale and a treatise on racial harmony. With our highest-ever ratings, we found few negatives, although most people thought it lacked some credibility. Someone who knew the actual story said that many details of the film are untrue, and others said that the leadership style presented does not necessarily work well. But most of us loved the characters, the acting, the music, and the good-over-evil message. The discussion, of course, elicited all kinds of sports experiences—relationships with teammates and coaches, as well as racial difficulties. It also encouraged a long discussion about team building in other situations.

JANUARY 2001
CHOCOLAT
Average rating: 7.3
Range of ratings: 6 to 8

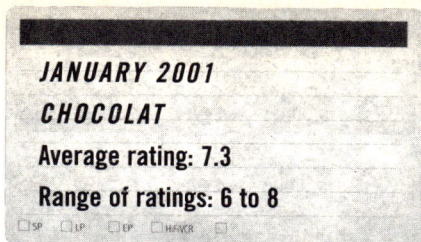

Lasse Hallström directed this quirky movie, starring Juliette Binoche as a young mother, Victoire Thivisol as her daughter, Judi Dench as an estranged grandmother, and Alfred Molina as an overly zealous mayor. The mother and daughter bring spiced chocolates to a repressed, religious French town in the late 1950s, upsetting the equilibrium of all the townspeople. The exotic sweets fill voids in many people's lives, and their behavior changes as a result. The mayor tries to get rid of the newcomers not only because they purvey chocolate treats during Lent but especially because the woman is having an affair and is shaking people up about sex. There are very funny and very poignant moments in this film, and most of us liked it very much. We noted the fine acting, interesting characters, good use of music, and the original storyline. However, some people said that it is rather contrived, and we agreed that it is really a fable. One woman said, in fact, that she hated it the first time she saw it because the pieces didn't fit, but then she read a review labeling it a fable and loved it on a second viewing. We talked about repressed towns we have lived in and judgmental people we have known. This led into the issues of nudity and coarse language in films, and some women said that they are less offended than they used to be. The consensus was that we still want to be exposed to all types of good films—whatever elements that may entail.

MARCH 2001
THE WIDOW OF ST. PIERRE
Average rating: 8.1
Range of ratings: 7 to 9
☐ SP ☐ LP ☐ EP ☐ HI/WCR ☐

This is a drama in French (with subtitles) from director Patrice Leconte. Set in 1850, a fisherman (Emir Kusturica) who has committed a brutal murder is sent to prison on the French Canadian island of St. Pierre. He is scheduled to die by the guillotine, but he is befriended by the wife (Juliette Binoche) of the man in charge. The commandant loves his wife and fears losing her, so he indulges her requests to help the condemned man. The crime had been done in a drunken stupor, and the prisoner's humanity comes through in many ways—especially through a sexy scene in the greenhouse. Because the prisoner later shows heroism and saves lives, many people would like to free him, but tough decisions must be made. We all found this tense story compelling. Many of us actually felt cold while watching the barren, snow-covered terrain. The color and cinematography are gorgeous. But some of us hated the unhappy ending, and that pushed us into a discussion of how we *wanted* it to end. We also explored our feelings about capital punishment, including how those feelings have changed or remained the same over our lifetime. It was fascinating to hear who and what may have influenced our ideas about the death penalty.

MAY 2001

MEMENTO

Average rating: 6.3

Range of ratings: zero to 9

☐ SP   ☐ LP   ☐ EP   ☐ HFIVCR   ☐

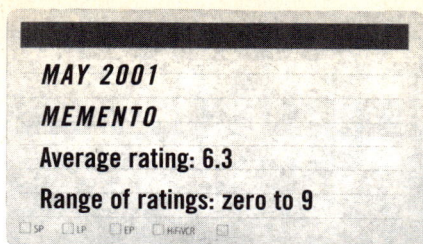

This thriller from writer and director Christopher Nolan is about a memory-impaired man who is out to avenge the murder of his wife. The gimmick is that the story is told backward, starting at the climax and working scene by scene to the beginning. Guy Pearce plays the pathetic victim-hero, who must write things on notes, objects, or his body in order to have any history or plan. It has a neo-film-noir quality. Many of us "got" this film, but a lot of us didn't. People on the positive side found it unique and engrossing—something they will definitely see again. Two of us thought that the unclear nature of "truth" provoked a lot of thought. The theme, to a few people, was the chaotic nature of twentieth-century culture as it struggles with sensory overload and short-term memory loss. The rest of us got upset because we couldn't figure the film out. It gave two of us a headache, and one man said that the messages the other members explained weren't worth figuring out anyway. This was one of those fun evenings when we almost came to blows. We wondered whether we had seen the same movie. There were a few insults about intelligence and a few replies about backward-type thinking. We talked about differences in people's thinking patterns (linear versus chaotic) and the split between those of us who love figuring out external, action-filled mysteries versus those of us who prefer to think about psychological, internal mysteries.

JUNE 2001
THE LUZHIN DEFENSE
Average rating: 7.3
Range of ratings: 6 to 8
☐ SP ☐ LP ☐ EP ☐ HFWCR ☐ I

Dutch filmmaker Marleen Gorris based this project on Vladimir Nabokov's 1930 Russian-language novel, *The Defense*. It is a character study focused around the game of chess, with John Turturro as the emotionally inadequate champion and Emily Watson as his muse and savior. They are an unlikely couple, and her very proper parents are against the union. But both young people seem obsessed as their relationship flows through match after match, with many obstructions and a breakup along the way. His former teacher is particularly cruel and treacherous. This is an unusual and intense film, and it was interesting to learn about the world of chess. The acting is fabulous—especially Turturro, who plays an odd mix of genius and idiot. The cinematography is great, too, with beautiful, 1920s European locations and lavish costumes and interiors. The flashbacks are very effective in helping us under-stand the chess player's psychology. On the negative side, however, we thought that some scenes were overplayed for melodrama, and a few of the plot points were illogical. We explored which people among us like chess, how many of us find it intolerable, and what an interest in chess might or might not mean about one's personality and character.

JULY 2001

A.I. (ARTIFICIAL INTELLIGENCE)
Average rating: 4.7
Range of ratings: 1 to 9
☐ SP ☐ LP ☐ EP ☐ HFHVCR ☐

This is Steven Spielberg's realization of an unfinished science-fiction project from the late Stanley Kubrick. Haley Joel Osment plays both a real boy and the model for a robot, while Frances O'Connor is his mother. The robot has been programmed to love his mother deeply, but this creates problems when the real boy comes out of his coma. Weird robotic characters play lifelike games with real people. There is a wild group of gangsterlike creatures, accompanied by loud, driving music. And the ending involves underwater activities. We were not alone in giving this film rather low ratings. It had been eagerly anticipated and was a big disappointment to many critics. Most of our group thought it was well done technically, with state-of-the-art special effects. Some of us also found the parent-child story to be touching and engrossing. Generally, the sci-fi lovers among us were positive. But most of us said it didn't work for us. Among the words used were *trite, silly, nonsense, nothing original, garbage,* and *boring.* We thought that perhaps the transition from Kubrick's concept to Spielberg's realization was too difficult. Spielberg reportedly wanted to honor his friend, but the result feels like two or three different movies—and not very good ones at that. We segued into a discussion of some other Kubrick movies, especially *Eyes Wide Shut,* about which the group was also mostly negative. The parent-child story got some attention, with the women more interested in this than the men.

AUGUST 2001
THE CLOSET
Average rating: 7.3
Range of ratings: 6 to 9
☐ SP ☐ LP ☐ EP ☐ HI-FI/VCR ☐

This French (with subtitles) comedy stars Daniel Auteuil as an accountant who has worked for the same company for years and Gérard Depardieu as his nemesis. The company is a contraceptive manufacturer, so that suggests some of the jokes. Auteuil, an ineffectual man, learns that he is about to lose his job in a downsizing, and he becomes suicidal. But his psychologist neighbor, a gay man, hatches a scheme whereby the powers that be will think Auteuil is gay and thus be unwilling to fire him. It works. His demeaning ex-wife and son gain new respect for him. His tough female boss suddenly finds him sexy. Funniest of all, a macho coworker becomes confused about his own sexual identity and begins to hit on Auteuil. Most of us loved this laugh-out-loud movie. We found it delightfully French. We especially liked its ability to look comically at prejudice and pomposity. But some people saw it as sitcom-ish—nothing deep. We wished the two villains had been punished more. Our discussion about homosexuality got a bit heated, with two of the men hating what they see as special treatment for gays in the workplace. This film does reinforce the impression that gays must be treated with kid gloves in order for an employer to avoid litigation. The women seemed less strident about homosexuality in general.

SEPTEMBER 2001

INNOCENCE

Average rating: 7.8

Range of ratings: 4 to 9.9

☐ SP ☐ LP ☐ EP ☐ HiFi/VCR ☐

A low-budget Australian film, the focus here is on rediscovered passion in one's later years. Julia Blake plays the central character, who must choose between her long-term husband and her first love, who has recently sought her out. The story of the two lovers is told partly in flashbacks, and one gets a sense that they should have been together all these years. Her husband is shown to be neglectful and selfish, although their son does his best to intercede. Romance between people this age is seldom seen on screen, and this film is quite sensual. For example, Blake's character is in rapture as she listens to her lover play the church organ. The two members of our group who gave it low ratings said that the story is slow and depressing. It did not elucidate anything for them. The rest of us, however, found it interesting and moving. Some of us had shed tears as we watched it. We liked the supportive adult child–parent relationships, and we thought that the story seemed real. Some of us mentioned that the lover seems selfish, knowing what he does about his future. And we wished that there were a better ending, but we couldn't think of a realistic one. Several men felt sorry for the jilted husband, and a couple of women thought that Blake's character could have made a better life with him if she had tried harder. We told some stories of late-life love among our parents or friends, and we acknowledged that it *can* be a disaster. But we also talked about how hard it is to get old without love in one's life. People long for passion at any age.

OCTOBER 2001
BREAD AND TULIPS
Average rating: 7.7
Range of ratings: 5 to 9.8

This is an Italian (subtitled) film directed by Silvio Soldini. Licia Maglietta plays a bored, dutiful housewife with two teenage sons. She is suddenly separated from her group during a family vacation in Venice, and she tries to return home, but then she takes advantage of her freedom to rediscover herself. Her husband is a plumbing supplier, with her sister-in-law as his mistress. He doesn't appreciate his wife until she is gone. Eventually, he hires an amateur detective to find her, but she is moving on. She befriends both men and women in her new location, and she finds a job as well as romance. Her dilemma is between her maternal instinct and her desire to find the self that she lost so many years ago. In our group, those who loved it cited her right to leave this useless family. The story speaks to the questions most of us have in our heads about whether we have missed chances in life and whether we will know the good opportunities when they do arrive. The film is funny, and it's symbolic of the state of many marriages. Then, there were others among us who hated the message that it is okay to leave one's family. These people found the film slow and trite. Any laughter they heard in the theater felt forced. Our discussion included a few innuendoes that this is dangerous territory. We were able to hit the general topics of the need for communication and not taking partners for granted, but this evening ended uncharacteristically early.

DECEMBER 2001
AMÉLIE
Average rating: 7.5
Range of ratings: 4 to 9
SP LP EP H-F/VCR

Amélie is a French romantic comedy with English subtitles. It was directed by Jean-Pierre Jeunet, and its increasingly famous star is Audrey Tautou. A young woman who has had a difficult childhood goes to work as a waitress in a Paris café. She finds a box of treasures hidden in her apartment and sets out to find its rightful owner. Thus begin her efforts to transform the lives of her friends and neighbors, as well as her father's. Eventually, she finds love herself, and she is quite resourceful about making that relationship work. There are some magical and fantasy elements here, and the film has been called a fable. Most of us loved the creativity and sense of fun in this movie. It is charming and clever—a feel-good, imaginative work of art. The Amélie character is full of joy and energy. The cinematography is a love letter to Paris. Four of us, however, were not impressed. They thought that Amélie was a silly, immature girl and that the movie was much too long. Everyone did agree that the scenes of courtship in the café are priceless. We spent some time trying to ferret out why the Amélie character was so appealing to some and so appalling to others. There were stories from women members of girlhood traumas with girls like this character, and there were suggestions from the men that they had dated girls like this. The conclusion was that our reactions to this girl were somewhat irrational and very idiosyncratic.

NEW YEAR'S EVE 2001
THE ROYAL TENENBAUMS
Average rating: 7.4
Range of ratings: 5 to 10
☐ SP ☐ LP ☐ EP ☐ HF/VCR ☐

Wes Anderson is the talented young director of this farce about a dysfunctional family of geniuses. The cast includes Gene Hackman, Anjelica Huston, Danny Glover, Ben Stiller, Gwyneth Paltrow, and Owen Wilson. We see the kids grow from their childish antics to their reluctant, chaotic adulthoods. We see the parents through a divorce into slightly more mature adjustments. Most of us enjoyed this for what it is—a hilarious black comedy. We did not mind that the characters are one-dimensional and too exaggerated to be real. But some of us expected much more from this cast. Some said that the laughter in the theater seemed forced, and two people thought that the film is eminently forgettable. "Family" was our topic for the evening, and everyone was glad not to have grown up in this one. We talked about determining when one has to cut ties and when one must find ways to make a family work. And we mentioned the curse of being a genius. Most of us with kids had thought at one time that we might have one of those, but we soon learned how wrong we were—and were grateful for that!

MARCH 2002
MONSOON WEDDING
Average rating: 7.9
Range of ratings: 4 to 10
☐ SP ☐ LP ☐ EP ☐ HF/VCR ☐

This is a "Bollywood" (the Indian film industry based in Bombay) film in English, Hindi, and Punjabi. The director is Mira Nair, and the cast includes many of India's biggest stars. The story is built around an extended family that gathers for the arranged marriage of their daughter to an engineer from America. Along with the celebration, the family confronts dark secrets of abuse and illicit affairs. The bride's father must finally choose between morality and family loyalty. There is also a charming romance between the wedding planner and a family servant. Most of us loved this movie for its joyous exuberance and family issues. The scenes of the young couple getting to know each other are wonderfully written. The dysfunctions in the family are probably typical of most families. The comedy is deft, and the cinematography is fabulous. The use of music and movement is uniquely engaging. Our three low ratings were given by people who thought the film was chaotic. So much was going on all the time that one man felt claustrophobic. Another man said that the film is totally forgettable; the family members don't seem at all real. We learned that three of our group members have been to big weddings in India, and their descriptions were very interesting. They talked about how important weddings are to families there and how graciously they were treated as outsiders. There were a few tales of family weddings among our group, but the major discussion focused on arranged marriages. Most of us thought that they have advantages over the current love-based system, but we agreed that Americans, including ourselves and our kids, could never accept that kind of control from our parents.

APRIL 2002
CHANGING LANES
Average rating: 8.6
Range of ratings: 8 to 10
SP   LP   EP   HH/HCR

Roger Michell directed this big-budget Hollywood movie, starring Ben Affleck and Samuel L. Jackson. It is the story of a young, high-powered attorney and a down-on-his-luck recovering alcoholic whose paths cross in an auto accident. Both of them have bad tempers, and their lives are shown in parallel tracks as their rage escalates. The good and the bad of New York City provide the background for the plot. Both of these men have messy personal lives, and both of them are struggling with moral dilemmas. Our group seldom chooses this kind of blockbuster film, but we are glad we did. The script, by Chap Taylor, is smart, and the acting is first-rate—certainly the best performance ever for Ben Affleck. The scenes with his wife and his father-in-law (Sydney Pollack), especially, show fascinating moral complexity. The wives' roles are small, but both women are strong. The characters seem real. The issues have the ring of truth and humanity. We cared about these people. The combination of all this with exciting action scenes is truly unusual, and we were all surprised at how much we liked it. We talked about the definitions of success—how hard that concept is to define, let alone accomplish. This film reminded one woman of *Election* and the issue of ends versus means. We also focused on the ending, and we differed on whether the young lawyer would (or should) stay with his wife, with the girlfriend, or with neither of them.

JUNE 2002

UNFAITHFUL

Average rating: 7.6

Range of ratings: 5 to 9

☐ SP ☐ LP ☐ EP ☐ HF/VCR ☐

An erotic drama-thriller, *Unfaithful* was directed by Adrian Lyne. It stars Richard Gere as the husband, Diane Lane as his wife, and Olivier Martinez as the young French lover. It is loosely based on the 1969 film *La Femme Infidele,* directed by Claude Chabrol. After eleven years of marriage, a businessman, his homemaker-volunteer wife, and their son seem happily ensconced in the suburbs. Then, quite by accident, she falls into the arms of a young Frenchman and begins an obsessive sexual affair. When the husband eventually suspects, he engages a private investigator, setting into motion a series of acts that leave him and his wife reeling. Most of us liked the symbolism in this film, from the bike tipping over at the house to the green-yellow-red traffic light at the end. We liked Gere in a role against type, and we all agreed that Lane's performance was magnificent. Most of us liked the lack of explanations for her acts, although some of us thought there should have been more motivation shown. One woman saw Gere as a boob who couldn't get his sweater or socks on straight, and she thought that Lane had lots of reasons to stray. Two of our group, who gave the film its lower ratings, focused on the immorality of Lane's acts. One person hated the juxtaposition of the first half, which focused on relationship details, with the second half, which was largely action. It felt like two different movies to him. The ending elicited a lot of discussion, and we were divided into three possible outcomes. In the general discussion, we wondered about why so many men are successful in business but clueless in their personal lives.

Some people thought that the husband's actions are realistic, while others thought that a man like this would never be so out of control. Someone raised Lyne's other films, *Fatal Attraction* and *Indecent Proposal,* saying how much good grist these movies have been for dinner-table conversations. Realizing that sex is dangerous territory, we talked about the range we've seen in relationships—from totally closed, where there is divorce or even murder if one person strays, to open marriages. Without getting too specific, we found that we probably have that range within our own group.

AUGUST 2002
ROAD TO PERDITION
Average rating: 7
Range of ratings: 5 to 9

☐ SP   ☐ LP   ☐ EP   ☐ HFG/CR   ☐

This is an unusual gangster film, starring Tom Hanks and Paul Newman. The details of the Depression-era midwest are meticulously portrayed, and the boy who plays Hanks's young son is phenomenal—especially for a novice. Despite the emphasis on family, however, this is a brutal, violent movie. The few of us who loved it commented on the feeling of authenticity and the good acting. But many of us were disappointed in a film that has been so widely hyped. The Catholic church comes across as hypocritical and almost criminal, even though many psychopaths do indeed fit religion into their psychopathy. The story is surprisingly cold, and few of us could identify with any of the characters. Hanks's character was a terrible parent, and his wife was an ineffectual mother. Several scenes were unrealistic, including the son driving the getaway car. We liked the ending, although it was terribly sad. Discussion focused on our members' father-son relationships. We also talked about religion and the many current difficulties in the Catholic church. This film was compared to *The Godfather* and other gangster movies, and the others were considered superior.

SEPTEMBER 2002
MY BIG FAT GREEK WEDDING
Average rating: 7.3
Range of ratings: 5 to 9

☐ SP ☐ LP ☐ EP ☐ HF/VCR ☐

There was almost more discussion of the way this indie film got made (through the money and influence of Rita Wilson and Tom Hanks) than the movie itself, but that is a great story of persistence and luck. Nia Vardalos wrote the screenplay and starred, hiring John Corbett to play her boyfriend. It is a joyful comedy about family and culture. Many people said they laughed out loud. They liked the difficult yet supportive family and thought the mother and father should both get supporting Oscars. The Windex scenes are hilarious. The dialogue is wonderful. But two people said that this film is silly and superficial. One man said that it does not qualify for our usual level of discussion, but we all agreed that a feel-good movie is needed from time to time. We talked at length about how much control parents should have over their children, especially over whom their child should marry. Not surprisingly, the line "The man is the head of the house, but the woman is the neck" got lots of reaction.

NOVEMBER 2002

BARBERSHOP

Average rating: 7.9

Range of ratings: 6 to 8.5

☐ SP ☐ LP ☐ EP ☐ HFA/CR ☐

Ice Cube produced and stars in this comedy, with a primarily black cast. The film's setting is the very rundown South Side of Chicago, and it has a lively, frenetic pace. The main character has inherited a barbershop, where most of the action takes place, but he has no use for it and all that the place means until he almost loses it in a get-rich-quick scheme. Overall, the group felt that this film, with its hip-hop language, is very effective in teaching lessons about life. It is well written, directed, and acted. It is a change of pace for many moviegoers, and it depicts various aspects of Chicago's diverse black culture. On the negative side, some of our members found it hard to relate to, and one man thought the black stereotypes were wrong. The group joked about dreams most of us have had for getting rich quickly and the ways in which we have been disabused of those ideas by our family and culture. There was some discussion about the criticisms that have been made of this film by Jesse Jackson and other black leaders. Most people felt that the film's handling of black historical incidents is healthy and that Jackson's criticisms will only help the film to be seen by more people.

DECEMBER 2002

FAR FROM HEAVEN

Average rating: 6.8

Range of ratings: 3 to 9

☐ SP ☐ LP ☐ EP ☐ HFA/CR ☐

Set in suburban Connecticut in 1957, this film stars Julianne Moore, Dennis Quaid, and Dennis Haysbert. It is directed by Todd Haynes in the style of a 1950s melodrama, but our group agreed that it could never have been made at that time. The themes of family secrets and interracial love would not have been acceptable. The cinematography, especially the use of color, is wonderful, and the acting is superb, but our ratings were diverse. Those who loved the film mentioned the music and the fascinating relationships. Those who hated it thought the music was overdone and the characters and plot were quite unrealistic. Most of us talked about where we were and what we were doing in 1957, and we compared notes about our experiences vis-à-vis family, race, and homosexuality at that time. We talked about which partner was more at fault in this movie relationship, and several people were critical of Moore's actions with the gardener. The women lamented Moore's friends, who did not stick by her, and we thought that the women's friendships would be stronger today.

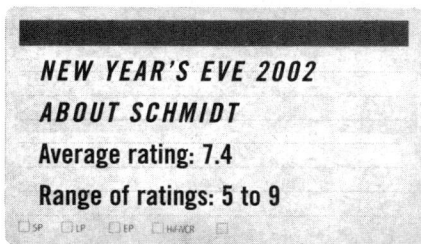

NEW YEAR'S EVE 2002
ABOUT SCHMIDT
Average rating: 7.4
Range of ratings: 5 to 9

☐ SP   ☐ LP   ☐ EP   ☐ HFMXR   ☐

This is a darkly comedic character study of a sixty-six-year-old retired insurance executive in Nebraska. Jack Nicholson gives a stellar performance, as does Kathy Bates. The man's wife dies suddenly, and he must learn to cope with his loss, their daughter's wedding, and all his regrets over a period of a few weeks. The device used to indicate his thoughts is his letters to a foster child in Africa. Those who loved this movie found it creative and funny.

Nicholson's facial expressions were priceless. But some people thought that Nicholson was wrong for the part. One woman said that all the characters were very shallow, and two men found only absurd humor. The letter from the foster child at the end seemed, to some of us, sad and unrealistic rather than hopeful. The film did provoke discussions of retirement difficulties, as well as the fact that we often don't appreciate people until they are gone. We also talked about how hard it is when your child marries a person you don't like. We admired the Nicholson character's handling of the wedding speech, and we were relieved that he had no epiphany about the marriage. He still called the groom a nincompoop at the end.

JANUARY 2003
ADAPTATION
Average rating: 6.1
Range of ratings: 4 to 9

Nicolas Cage plays a neurotic, blocked screenwriter, who is trying to adapt a book about orchids, and he also plays his more confident twin brother. Meryl Streep and Chris Cooper give great performances as the book's author and its subject—the orchid expert. Our group was split between those who loved this weird, engaging story and those who thought it makes no sense. Everyone gave the acting high marks. The general discussion initially focused on orchids. We found that two of our members have intense interest in this subject, and they added to the group's knowledge base. Then we talked about the relationship between Streep and Cooper. Most of the men thought the drug use and love affair were unrealistic, while some of the women saw the attraction in this "bad boy." There was also some discussion regarding caring too much about what others think versus not caring at all—the major difference between the two brothers. The middle ground is where most of us find ourselves, but the effect of age on this quality is positive. Most of us gain confidence and comfort along with our wrinkles.

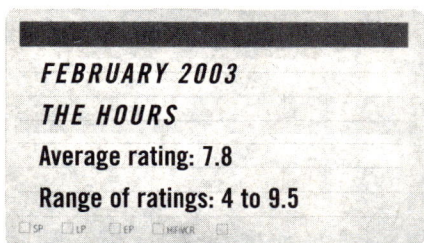

FEBRUARY 2003
THE HOURS
Average rating: 7.8
Range of ratings: 4 to 9.5
☐ SP ☐ LP ☐ EP ☐ HIFIVCR ☐

This is the story of Virginia Woolf and two women who were later influenced by her writings. We all agreed that the acting by Nicole Kidman, Julianne Moore, Meryl Streep, and Ed Harris is superb, but our other reactions were somewhat gender-based: More women loved it than men did, but two men also rated it very high. The positives include the interesting explorations of women's societal roles in relation to husbands and children and the clear dramatizations of depression. Things are better now, with many more choices for women, but navigating toward the right balance is still difficult. Most of us liked the twist that connected two characters at the end. On the negative side, however, several people found this film slow, boring, and too depressing. Two men said that the women all had nice, supportive partners, and they should have been able to snap out of it. Moore's darling little boy deserved better parenting. Besides the discussion of women's roles in the past and present, we focused on the cause of depression. Is it situational and reactive or biochemically caused? We shared some personal experiences and concluded that depression is primarily biochemical. We discussed what we know about suicide and segued into what we might do to help a suicidal friend or family member.

APRIL 2003
THE PIANIST
Average rating: 8.9
Range of ratings: 7 to 10

☐ SP   ☐ LP   ☐ EP   ☐ HFWCR   ☐

This is the compelling true story of a pianist, Wladyslaw Szpilman, who survived the most horrific Nazi atrocities in Warsaw. The group agreed that Roman Polanski's Academy Award for best director was richly deserved, as was Adrien Brody's recognition as best actor. Most of us said that we might not have seen the film without the group assignment because it sounded so grim, but the experience was thrilling and memorable for most of us. The only negative comments were that this has been seen before in films like *Schindler's List* and that there was little character development for the supporting cast. However, most of our members marveled at the development of the mood—from pleasant, middle-class life to incredible deprivation and desperation. It is also significant, in contrast to other holocaust films, that no concentration camp is ever seen here. The sets and cinematography are brilliant. The feeling is amazingly balanced between man's inhumanity and his humanity toward others. The moment that Brody's character plays the piano inaudibly is beautiful, and we all loved the music that played through the end credits, during which few audience members left. There was considerable discussion of Roman Polanski's life history and some disagreement about whether his crime should keep him from re-entering the United States. One man listed the atrocities that have continued to occur around the world since World War II. A woman recounted her uncontrollable trembling while watching this film and for hours afterward. We talked about our good luck to have been raised in the United States, but we also discussed the feeling of more vulnerability since 9/11. We ended with a spirited disagreement about how the word *pianist* should be pronounced.

CHAPTER 17

OTHER VIDEO SUGGESTIONS

Instead of going to see first-run films in theaters, movie groups may choose to rent videos or DVDs because of lower cost, convenience, distance to big-city theaters, or other factors. Movie groups may also be formed around a theme, which requires the video format. For example, a group in New York City decided to have a Jane Austen "Emmathon," watching three versions of *Emma* (including *Clueless*) over one weekend and feasting on cucumber sandwiches and tea. Another group might do a Shakespeare series, or films about race, or animal subjects, or great loves, or old black-and-white films, or thrillers, or screwball comedies, or one director's or one actor's body of work. These themes can only be explored with the help of a good video store or an online video source.

Therefore, in addition to the previous chapter's list and ratings of the movies that our group has seen, this chapter suggests several categories of films. Each group of movies is followed by five questions, which should be useful in stimulating group discussions.

A few of our favorites from chapter 16 reappear in these lists, and each group is in alphabetical order—not in any order of our preference. We have tried *not* to include obscure or very old films, which would be hard to find in rental stores, but we have included a few classics that should be available. No animated films are mentioned.

There are many sources available for more information about these films. Books like Zagat's new *Movie Guide* will give people synopses and opinions. Internet sites are also convenient.

We have focused here on films that would be suitable for group discussions, but we hope that this information will be useful for individuals and couples as well.

CHICK FLICKS

- ▶ *An Affair to Remember*, 1957
- ▶ *Breakfast at Tiffany's*, 1961
- ▶ *The Bridges of Madison County*, 1995
- ▶ *Enchanted April*, 1992
- ▶ *The First Wives' Club*, 1996
- ▶ *The Hours*, 2002
- ▶ *Sense and Sensibility*, 1995
- ▶ *Steel Magnolias*, 1989
- ▶ *Thelma and Louise*, 1991
- ▶ *The Way We Were*, 1973

Questions:

1. Is this film more appealing to women than to men? If so, why?

2. Which character do I most identify with? Why?

3. What does this script have to say about women's relationships with one another?

4. What is the quantity and quality of my relationships with other women?

5. How might I make these relationships richer?

GUY STUFF

- ▶ *Apollo 13*, 1995
- ▶ *Bull Durham*, 1988
- ▶ *Chariots of Fire*, 1981
- ▶ *Das Boot* (German), 1982
- ▶ *The French Connection*, 1971
- ▶ *Goodfellas*, 1990
- ▶ *Hoop Dreams*, 1994
- ▶ *The Hunt for Red October*, 1990
- ▶ *Raging Bull*, 1980
- ▶ *The Usual Suspects*, 1995

Questions:

1. Is this movie more appealing to men than to women? If so, why?

2. What does this film have to say about the life of a man versus that of a woman?

3. What actions in this film are interesting to me? What emotions? Why?

4. How have my family and working experiences influenced my relationships with other men?

5. What do I enjoy about being with other men? What do I fear or dislike? How could I make my relationships with men stronger?

ROMANCE AND SEX

▶ *Bob and Carol and Ted and Alice*, 1969

▶ *Body Heat*, 1981

▶ *Boogie Nights*, 1997

▶ *Breaking the Waves*, 1996

▶ *Carnal Knowledge*, 1971

▶ *Casablanca*, 1942

▶ *Cat on a Hot Tin Roof*, 1958

▶ *Fatal Attraction*, 1987

▶ *Four Weddings and a Funeral*, 1994

▶ *In the Company of Men*, 1997

▶ *Jerry Maguire*, 1996

▶ *Last Tango in Paris* (French), 1973

▶ *Leaving Las Vegas*, 1995

▶ *Sex, Lies, and Videotape*, 1989

▶ *The Sure Thing*, 1985

▶ *Two for the Road*, 1967

▶ *Unfaithful*, 2002

▶ *An Unmarried Woman*, 1978

▶ *War of the Roses*, 1989

▶ *When Harry Met Sally*, 1989

▶ *Who's Afraid of Virginia Woolf?*, 1966

Questions:

1. How would I describe this film's core relationship?
2. How healthy or unhealthy is this relationship? Why?
3. What is the role of sex in this relationship? In most relationships?
4. How does the relationship in this film change over time? How do I feel about that?
5. What is my experience with romantic and sexual relationships? What could I do to strengthen this area of my life?

FATHERS AND DAUGHTERS, FATHERS AND SONS

▶ *About Schmidt*, 2002
▶ *Affliction*, 1998
▶ *Billy Elliott*, 2000
▶ *In the Bedroom*, 2001
▶ *Say Anything*, 1989
▶ *Sleepless in Seattle*, 1993
▶ *Ulee's Gold*, 1997

MOTHERS AND DAUGHTERS, MOTHERS AND SONS

▶ *Antonia's Line* (Dutch), 1995
▶ *E.T. (The Extra-Terrestrial)*, 1982
▶ *The Joy Luck Club*, 1993
▶ *Ordinary People*, 1980
▶ *Secrets and Lies*, 1996
▶ *Terms of Endearment*, 1983

Questions:

1. What is the parent-child relationship all about in this film?
2. How healthy or unhealthy is it? Why?
3. How does the relationship change over time in this story? Is the change interesting and believable?
4. What is the nature of my relationships with my parents and with my children?
5. What might I do to strengthen these? What are the potential risks and benefits for me in these changes?

OTHER RELATIONSHIPS

▶ *American Beauty*, 1999

▶ *Atlantic City*, 1981

▶ *The Big Chill*, 1983

▶ *The Birdcage*, 1996

▶ *The Brothers McMullen*, 1995

▶ *Chocolat*, 2000

▶ *The Crying Game*, 1992

▶ *Deliverance*, 1972

▶ *The Dinner Game* (French), 1999

▶ *Driving Miss Daisy*, 1989

▶ *Easy Rider*, 1969

▶ *The Fabulous Baker Boys*, 1989

▶ *Fanny and Alexander* (Swedish), 1983

▶ *Five Easy Pieces*, 1970

▶ *Hannah and Her Sisters*, 1986

▶ *The Horse Whisperer*, 1998

- ▶ *Kolya* (Czech and Russian), 1996
- ▶ *Kramer vs. Kramer*, 1979
- ▶ *The Last Picture Show*, 1971
- ▶ *Midnight Cowboy*, 1969
- ▶ *Monsoon Wedding*, 2002
- ▶ *My Dinner with Andre*, 1981
- ▶ *Out of Africa*, 1985
- ▶ *The Player*, 1992
- ▶ *A River Runs Through It*, 1992
- ▶ *Scent of a Woman*, 1992
- ▶ *You Can Count on Me*, 2000

Questions:

1. What are the central and peripheral relationships in this story? To what extent are they healthy or unhealthy? Why?

2. Were the characters well cast? In what ways did the actors enhance or diminish the story?

3. Did the conflict between the characters get resolved satisfactorily? How might I have changed the script?

4. What is the role of family in my life? The role of friends? To what extent are they the same or different?

5. Whom can I count on in life? Who can count on me? Are there any relationships on which I need to work harder?

COMING OF AGE

- ▶ *Almost Famous*, 2000
- ▶ *American Graffiti*, 1973
- ▶ *The Breakfast Club*, 1985
- ▶ *Breaking Away*, 1979
- ▶ *Clueless*, 1995
- ▶ *Heathers*, 1989
- ▶ *Rushmore*, 1998
- ▶ *Summer of '42*, 1971

Questions:

1. What are the major issues these characters face in growing up?
2. Why is life so hard for adolescents? What might these characters do differently?
3. How difficult were my teenaged years? Why?
4. Looking back, what might I have done differently in the context of growing up?
5. In what ways do my adolescent experiences still affect the person that I am today?

THE AGING PROCESS

- ▶ *Cocoon*, 1985
- ▶ *Cookie's Fortune*, 1999
- ▶ *Harold and Maude*, 1972
- ▶ *Innocence*, 2001
- ▶ *On Golden Pond*, 1981

Questions:

1. What attitudes do these characters have about aging? To what extent are their ideas healthy or unhealthy? Why?
2. Do these people accept aging gracefully or fight it with all their might? Where do most people I know fit on this continuum?
3. In what ways has life beat these people up? In what ways has life been good to them?
4. How will I face (or how am I facing) the aging process?
5. What have been my familial examples for aging? How would I like to do it differently?

PHYSICAL HEALTH AND ILLNESS

▶ *The Doctor*, 1991
▶ *The Elephant Man*, 1980
▶ *Memento*, 2001
▶ *My Left Foot*, 1989
▶ *Philadelphia*, 1993

MENTAL HEALTH AND ILLNESS

▶ *As Good As It Gets*, 1997
▶ *Awakenings*, 1990
▶ *Days of Wine and Roses*, 1963
▶ *Girl, Interrupted*, 1999
▶ *Network*, 1976
▶ *One Flew Over the Cuckoo's Nest*, 1975
▶ *Postcards from the Edge*, 1990

▶ *Rain Man*, 1988
▶ *The Silence of the Lambs*, 1991
▶ *Sling Blade*, 1996

Questions:

1. What are the health issues for these characters? How do they handle their problems?
2. How does the health care system affect their recovery or lack of recovery? To what extent do these characters take responsibility for their own health?
3. In what ways do mental health issues differ from physical ones in our society? In most people's attitudes? In my own perspective?
4. How much do I help or hinder my own health? What can I do to improve my health?
5. What systems do I have in place to help others who may have healthcare needs or to get healthcare help when I need it?

SOCIAL ISSUES (CAPITAL PUNISHMENT, RACE, HOMOSEXUALITY, POLITICS, PROSTITUTION, DRUGS, RELIGION, WAR)

▶ *The Accused*, 1988
▶ *All the President's Men*, 1976
▶ *Apocalypse Now*, 1979
▶ *Boys Don't Cry*, 1999
▶ *Chinatown*, 1974

▶ *Dances with Wolves*, 1990

▶ *Dead Man Walking*, 1995

▶ *Far from Heaven*, 2002

▶ *Gods and Monsters*, 1998

▶ *The Gods Must Be Crazy*, 1981

▶ *Klute*, 1971

▶ *The Last Temptation of Christ*, 1985

▶ *Malcolm X*, 1992

▶ *Norma Rae*, 1979

▶ *The Pianist*, 2002

▶ *Remember the Titans*, 2000

▶ *Saving Private Ryan*, 1998

▶ *Schindler's List*, 1993

▶ *Silkwood*, 1983

▶ *Traffic*, 2000

Questions:

1. What is the major social issue portrayed in this film? How is it handled?

2. What social change takes place (or fails to take place) in the course of the film? Why or why not?

3. How do I feel about this issue? How do most other people feel about it? Am I in sync with most other people on this or different from them? Why?

4. How have my family members and friends influenced my opinions about this issue? To what extent am I open to new information? Am I an independent thinker regarding most social issues? Am I a critical thinker?

5. In what ways could I influence this social issue for the better? Do I care enough about this matter to get more involved? If so, how?

BIOGRAPHY

- ▶ *A Beautiful Mind*, 2001
- ▶ *Gandhi*, 1982
- ▶ *Henry V*, 1989
- ▶ *The Last Emperor*, 1987
- ▶ *Lawrence of Arabia*, 1962
- ▶ *A Man for All Seasons*, 1966
- ▶ *Mrs. Brown*, 1997
- ▶ *Patton*, 1970
- ▶ *Pollock*, 2000

Questions:

1. What were the core beliefs of this historical figure? How did this person live his or her life?
2. In what ways was this person tested in life? How did he or she respond? How should he or she have responded differently? What might have been the results?
3. What parallels are there between this person's life and mine? What can I learn from this film?
4. What issues would I write about in my autobiography? How satisfied am I with the way I am living my life?

5. What issues might someone close to me write about in my biography? How might others see my life differently than I do? Does this suggest the need for any change?

COMEDIES

- ▶ *Annie Hall*, 1977
- ▶ *Barbershop*, 2002
- ▶ *Blazing Saddles*, 1974
- ▶ *Broadcast News*, 1987
- ▶ *City Slickers*, 1991
- ▶ *Crimes and Misdemeanors*, 1989
- ▶ *Dirty Rotten Scoundrels*, 1988
- ▶ *The Full Monty*, 1997
- ▶ *The Graduate*, 1967
- ▶ *Life Is Beautiful* (Italian), 1998
- ▶ *M*A*S*H*, 1970
- ▶ *My Big Fat Greek Wedding*, 2002
- ▶ *Same Time, Next Year*, 1978
- ▶ *Tootsie*, 1982
- ▶ *Working Girl*, 1988

Questions:

1. What is funny—or not funny—about this film? The story? The characters? The acting? The props?
2. Why is comedy so often closely linked with tragedy?
3. Is my sense of humor in sync with the humor of most

other people? If it's different, in what ways? Does my humor tend to be kind or caustic?

4. Do I prefer comedic films that are more broad or more subtle? What does this imply about me?

5. What can I do to enhance my sense of humor in real life? Might I bring funny lines from films into my real-life conversations?

MUSICALS, MUSIC, DANCE

▶ *Amadeus*, 1984
▶ *Center Stage*, 2000
▶ *Chicago*, 2002
▶ *Fiddler on the Roof*, 1971
▶ *Moulin Rouge!*, 2001
▶ *Mr. Holland's Opus*, 1995
▶ *Shall We Dance?* (Japanese), 1997
▶ *Shine*, 1996
▶ *Strictly Ballroom*, 1992
▶ *West Side Story*, 1961

Questions:

1. Does the subject of this film fit well with the music or dance therein? Why or why not?

2. What would this story have been like without music or dance? Better or worse?

3. What do these characters portray through music or dance that could not have been communicated with words?

4. What in my background drives me to like or dislike this kind of film?

5. Is there anything that I would like to pursue in the worlds of music or dance—either as a spectator or a participant?

INTRIGUING DRAMAS

- ▶ *Bagdad Café* (aka *Out of Rosenheim*), 1988
- ▶ *Changing Lanes*, 2002
- ▶ *The Cider House Rules*, 1999
- ▶ *Cinema Paradiso* (Italian), 1988; director's cut, 2002
- ▶ *Citizen Kane*, 1941
- ▶ *Doctor Zhivago*, 1965
- ▶ *Election*, 1999
- ▶ *The English Patient*, 1996
- ▶ *The Godfather*, 1972
- ▶ *The Godfather, Part II*, 1974
- ▶ *Good Will Hunting*, 1997
- ▶ *Il Postino* (Italian), 1994
- ▶ *The Piano*, 1993
- ▶ *Quiz Show*, 1994
- ▶ *The Shawshank Redemption*, 1994
- ▶ *The Sweet Hereafter*, 1997
- ▶ *To Kill a Mockingbird*, 1962
- ▶ *Unforgiven*, 1992
- ▶ *Wall Street*, 1987

Questions:

1. What is this story really about? Was there an interesting problem or conflict that drew me in? How are the themes told through the characters?

2. What are the recognizable touches of the director? Are the actors effective in their roles? Was it an interesting setting?

3. Were there any troubling gaps or inconsistencies? Were there any scenes of special beauty or effectiveness?

4. What changes take place over time? How might I have altered the action or the ending?

5. Did the story inspire me? If so, in what way? What part of the story or characters do I relate to the most? Why?

Th-that's all, folks!

CONSULTATIONS

We hope that this book will give you any tools you might need to start your own group. This is our formula, honed over seven years, based on what works for us.

Instead of using our prescription, however, you may choose to invent your own rules and methods. Or, you may want to mix and match. Just as there is no perfect job, and there is no perfect partner, there surely is no perfect formula for a movie group. Whatever you do, we would love to hear about it (see the form provided on p. 191).

If you'd like some help, or if you don't want to rely only on this book, we have fourteen experts willing and able to provide consultations. We like to work in two-person teams, consisting of two men, two women, or a man and a woman, depending on the group you want to start. As of this writing, we have helped to start eight movie groups in various cities, and it has been a very rewarding experience for us.

You also might be interested in a talk to your corporation, trade association, college alumni group, etc., or perhaps you would like to suggest a media contact. It is our policy to provide help to senior citizens' groups or schools at very low cost.

Give us a call at (206) 236-2800 or check out our Web site: www.brookbaybooks.com.

Please send any and all comments to us, and let us know
if we may use them for future purposes. The address is:

FILMS AND FRIENDS
BROOK BAY BOOKS
8 BROOK BAY
MERCER ISLAND, WA 98040

_____

_____

_____

_____

_____

_____

_____

_____

_____

_____

_____

_____

_____

You may _____ may not _____ use my comments for future purposes.

Signature _____ Date _____

MOVIE GROUP RECORD

DATE: _____ HOSTS: _____

MOVIE TITLE: _____

MAJOR CAST/DIRECTOR: _____

RATING BY:

_____ ____   _____ ____

_____ ____   _____ ____

_____ ____   _____ ____

_____ ____   _____ ____

_____ ____   _____ ____

_____ ____   _____ ____

_____ ____   _____ ____

AVERAGE OF ALL RATINGS: _____

TYPICAL COMMENTS ABOUT THE MOVIE:

Positive:

Negative:

FUTURE DATES OR PLANS FOR THE GROUP:

ABOUT THE AUTHOR

Maryanne Vandervelde holds a Ph.D. from the University of Washington and a master's degree from the University of California at Berkeley. Her B.A. is from Calvin College.

As a psychologist, she worked fifteen years in clinical practice and then ran Pioneer Management, a corporate human resources consulting firm, for twenty years. With various corporations, she wrote, directed, and produced many training and development videos. She has also taught undergraduate and graduate students at the University of Washington, the University of Bridgeport, and other colleges. She hosted a radio show for three years in Connecticut.

Dr. Vandervelde has authored four other nonfiction books, including the bestselling *The Changing Life of the Corporate Wife,* and she has written many articles for the *Wall St. Journal,* the *New York Times,* professional journals, and popular periodicals. She also writes screenplays, one of which is now in development. She speaks regularly to corporate groups, trade associations, and nonprofit organizations. Her media appearances include *Today, Oprah, Hour Magazine,* and *CNN,* as well as other TV and radio programs.

She is married to H. Ray Looney, a retired corporate CEO. She has lived in Michigan, the Bay Area, New York City, Connecticut, and Washington State. Their adult son, Spencer Velde Looney, lives in Seattle.